D1322045

Texan's
Guide to
Consumer
Protection

Texan's
Guide to
Consumer
Protection

John L. Hill

Gulf Publishing Company
Book Division
Houston, London, Paris, Tokyo

Texan's Guide to Consumer Protection

Library of Congress Cataloging in Publication Data

Hill, John L   1923-
     Texan's guide to consumer protection.

     Includes index.
     1. Consumer protection—Texas. I. Title.
HC107.T43C634   381'.3   79-16767
ISBN 0-87201-132-1

The pronouns *he, him,* and *his* have been used in their traditional collective sense—applying both to the female and male genders—throughout this book. The author and the publisher recognize that the information in this book is as applicable to women as it is to men. No discrimination against either sex is intended in this publication.

Contents

Regulatory Agencies 104, Comptroller of the Currency 104, Federal Trade Commission 104

Acknowledgments

I gratefully acknowledge the assistance of many people in the preparation of this book. I especially want to thank David F. Bragg, Chief of the Attorney General's Consumer Protection Division, for his ideas, suggestions, and general editorial supervision of the manuscript. I also thank M. Debra Lowenthal and Barbara Marquardt, both of whom are Assistant Attorneys General in the Consumer Protection Division, for their excellent research and suggestions on the chapters on Insurance and Consumer Credit respectively.

Preface

On March 15, 1962, President Kennedy delivered a historic message to Congress on consumer protection. In this message, the President declared that our laws and our government should recognize four basic consumer rights:

1. *The right to safety*—to be protected against the marketing of goods which are hazardous to health or life.
2. *The right to be informed*—to be protected against fraudulent, deceitful, or grossly misleading information, advertising, labeling, or other practices, and to be given the facts (we) need to make an informed choice.
3. *The right to choose*—to be assured, wherever possible, access to a variety of products and services at competitive prices; and in those industries in which competition is not workable and Government regulation is substituted, an assurance of satisfactory quality and service at fair prices.
4. *The right to be heard*—to be assured that consumer interests will receive full and sympathetic consideration in the formulation of Government policy, and fair and expeditious treatment in its administrative tribunals.

These basic rights continue to be recognized by all responsible leaders as essential to the prosperity of our nation and the quality of our way of life. And, during the years that I had the privilege to serve as Attorney General of Texas, I worked to protect these rights.

As consumer protection has matured, however, we have found an additional right that needs to be added to the President's declaration. We must ensure consumers who have been harmed by unfair, deceptive, or dangerous practices the *right to an adequate and fair legal remedy*.

I believe in effective consumer protection. During 25 years of private law practice in Houston, I was regularly visited by people who had valid consumer complaints. And throughout those 25 years, I watched expressions of hope that something could be done turn quickly to frustration or anger when I explained that their complaints were very difficult to adequately address within the judicial system at that time.

Attorneys and lawsuits are expensive. A complaint involving several hundred dollars rarely justified the costs of turning the wheels of justice.

I learned then that something had to be done to more adequately open the courthouse doors to people with legitimate small claims. Their numbers were too great; and when added together, their losses translated into sums of money too large to ignore.

My experience in Houston also taught me that consumer protection is not only good for consumers, it also is good for business. People who fear deception and unfairness spend money reluctantly. The mutual trust that is essential between business and consumers will wither unless the victims of provable deception and unfairness are given the ability to redress their wrongs. Because of this, when people assume that a person who supports strong consumer protection efforts is against business, they are wrong. If you are for good consumer protection, you are for good business; if you are for good business, you are for good consumer protection. Indeed, good consumer protection laws should ensure that harassment and unjustified lawsuits are discouraged.

From being one of the least active states in 1972, Texas has become a leader in consumer protection. Our *Deceptive Trade Practices and Consumer Protection Act,* which prohibits all forms of misrepresentation in consumer transactions, is recognized nationwide as one of the strongest, and most effective tools for providing consumer *remedies* ever enacted. Many other statutes have been enacted since 1972 including the *Debt Collection Practices Act,* the *Home Solicitation Transactions* (Door-to-Door Sales) *Act* and several landlord-tenant acts.

But, consumer protection laws—though essential—are not enough. Unless consumers know about the important rights we now have, our consumer protection laws will gather dust and those who are defrauded and deceived will continue to lose money.

The purpose of this book is to provide the layperson with an easy-to-understand guide to consumer protection laws. We have tried to relate the laws to everyday transactions. My book will have served its purpose if, by reading it, more Texans learn their rights and guarantees under the consumer protection laws—and let these laws work for them.

John L. Hill
Austin, Texas
July, 1979

Buying Goods and Services

There are many, many different types of "consuming," but there is only one type that all of us do on a regular basis: buying goods and services. Personal consumption of goods and services is the backbone of the American economy. According to the U.S. Bureau of Economic Analysis, each year we spend more than $900 billion on goods and services.

Experience may be the best teacher, but in spite of our vast experience as purchasers of goods and services, we are still victimized by deception and other unlawful practices in the marketplace. The U.S. Chamber of Commerce estimates that victims of deceptive trade practices lose more than $21 *billion* annually.

With these facts in mind, this chapter considers certain key steps in the purchasing process not only to explain your rights under Texas and federal law as a purchaser, but also to alert you to some of the more frequently reported deceptive trade practices.

Advertising

In many cases advertisements are our first contact with a seller. We may be exposed to advertising in any number of ways. For instance, fre-

---

All lawsuits referred to in this book were filed by the Consumer Protection Division of the Office of the Attorney General of Texas, unless otherwise specified.

quently we seek out advertisements in order to evaluate which of the many brands of a product to buy. Even more frequently advertising seeks us out—on billboards, radio, television, and newspapers. In fact, it would be difficult indeed to avoid exposure to advertising.

Consider the case of television advertising alone. The average American watches approximately four hours of television a day. Of these four hours, one-and-one-half are during non-prime time, while the remaining two-and-one-half hours are viewed during prime time. The Federal Communications Commission (which regulates the television industry) allows advertisers to use eight minutes of each prime time hour of television for advertising. During non-prime time up to 12 minutes of each hour may be used for advertising. Most advertisements are 30 seconds in length; simple multiplication illustrates that the average American sees 75-80 television advertisements a day—or approximately 560 television advertisements each week! There is little doubt that advertising has assumed a significant place in our daily environment.

What is advertising? Simply stated, advertising is publicity; that is, publicity about a product or a service. What is the purpose of advertising? The answer to this question depends on your perspective.

A seller of goods or services would define advertising as a means by which consumers are *persuaded* to buy. A consumer, on the other hand, would define advertising as a means by which one is *informed* about a product or service. This difference in perspective is the root cause of most deceptive advertising. If sellers were more concerned about the informational rather than the persuasive aspects of advertising, consumers would be better equipped to shop wisely.

Noninformative Advertising

Noninformative advertising is carefully designed to give the impression of being factual even though no factual statements are made; in other words, an audio-visual "now you see it, now you don't."

Noninformative advertising is not caused by the advertisers' desire to evade telling the truth about their products. Instead, this type of advertising became popular when advertisers discovered that there was little objective difference between their products and those of competitors. By and large, coffee is coffee. Cigarettes are cigarettes. Medium-priced automobiles are medium-priced automobiles. There may be subjective differences; that is, one brand of coffee may *taste* better to some consumers than to others, but there is little objective difference for comparison.

Think of the day the wheel was invented. Now, imagine you are a prehistoric advertiser who has the job of advertising the invention. Would you choose a slogan like, "It rides smooth," or "The smooth curves of the wheel give it a stylish appearance?" Probably not. You would advertise the wheel by telling the one piece of factual information that makes the wheel superior to its competitor, the sled: "It Rolls!" Any advertiser today would do the same.

But what if your competitor begins to market a wheel? The factual ad—"It Rolls!"—no longer says your product is superior to the competitor's, since all wheels roll. Now you must find other factual differences which make your wheel superior to all others. Ultimately, all wheels (like cigarettes and coffee) will be about the same. At this point many advertisers turn to noninformative advertising.

There are as many different types of noninformative advertisements as there are advertisers. However, two types appear with such frequency that they deserve mention.

The first type avoids making any *direct* statements about a product or service. Consider the familiar toothpaste commercial that claims its brand "helps prevent cavities." The advertisement is noninformative because the same claim could be made about any other toothpaste—or, for that matter, about brushing your teeth *without* toothpaste. They also "help prevent cavities." Perhaps one product will help prevent cavities "better" than the other, but the claim made in the advertisement could lawfully be made about any toothpaste. The advertisement contains no information with which you can evaluate the product.

The second type of noninformative advertising makes claims that are so imprecise as to be useless. For instance, a national soap manufacturer once advertised that purchasing its brand of soap was "like getting one bar free." Obviously, if a consumer actually got one bar of soap free, the advertisement would proclaim this *fact* in big, bold letters. Or, if the soap lasted twice as long as other brands of soap, we would expect to see a direct statement to this effect. Instead we are told that purchasing the soap is *like* getting one bar free. This claim is so imprecise that no usable, factual information is imparted to the consumer.

There are many more examples of noninformative advertising, like the toothpaste that generates "sex appeal"; the soft drink that invites you to join its "generation"; or the mouthwash that proclaims itself to be a "breath deodorant" (aren't all mouthwashes?). The thing to remember about such advertising is that the advertiser is trying to get you to buy the advertisement instead of the product. "Sell the sizzle, not the steak" is an axiom of the advertising and promotion business. Since there is so little difference in quality among many products, the challenge to the advertiser today is to have an advertisement so appealing that people will buy the product in spite of its similarity to others.

So the message is, listen carefully to today's advertising. Buy the product—not the advertisement. Don't mentally supply "facts" that the advertiser is unable to supply in the advertisement.

Unlawful Advertising

The preceding section dealt with advertising techniques that are, for the most part, lawful. The sections that follow describe advertising practices that clearly are unlawful. While some of the practices mentioned may be new to you, many will be all too familiar.

False Advertising. This term encompasses many different unlawful practices. The general rule is: advertising must be *truthful*. That is, an advertiser cannot say a product is black if it is white. To illustrate, a Houston mattress company ran an advertisement containing a picture of a standard box springs and mattress set. This set was advertised for sale at a certain price. After receiving a number of consumer complaints, the Texas Attorney General's Consumer Protection Division determined that the pictured "box springs" foundation was actually a plywood box with no springs whatsoever. The advertisement was deemed false and a court order was obtained prohibiting similar advertising in the future.

State law also prohibits any advertising which has the "capacity or tendency" to deceive consumers. This standard applies to the advertisement as a whole, not just to one or two isolated pictures or words.

A chinchilla promotion company ran an advertisement that, in separate places, claimed (1) chinchillas may be raised in a spare room or garage, and (2) people who raise chinchillas can earn up to $10,000 a year. Each claim, read by itself, is true. It is *possible* to raise a limited number of chinchillas in a spare room or garage; and some chinchilla ranchers do earn up to $10,000 a year. When read together, however, the claims become false because no one raising chinchillas in a spare room or garage has made $10,000 a year. It is simply not possible to get the number of animals needed into so limited a space. Consequently, a court found the advertisement to be false.

Advertising also is false if it fails to say enough. Not only must an advertiser tell the truth; he must tell the *whole* truth. For instance, when General Motors Corporation ran out of Oldsmobile engines, it began substituting engines manufactured by another division. GM failed to disclose this substitution of engines to its customers. Accordingly, a successful lawsuit required GM to tell its customers the name of the manufacturer of the engines in their automobiles.

Bait-and-Switch Advertising. This type of advertising is defined as an attractive but *insincere* offer to sell a particular product at a certain price. The attractive offer is the "bait." When you respond to the offer, the seller usually disparages or talks down the advertised product, describing how it is not really a very good buy. Then the seller will try to sell you a more expensive product by describing its many virtues and advantages. The sales pitch and resulting purchase of the more expensive product comprise the "switch." Such advertising is unlawful because the insincere offer made by a seller in "bait" advertising tends to attract customers away from more honest sellers whose advertisements are genuine offers to sell their products. It also causes customers to buy more expensive products under misleading pretenses.

As an example, a nationwide retailer of home appliances advertised name-brand television sets at extremely attractive prices. When consumers responded, they found the advertised televisions out of adjustment and displaying generally poor pictures. Salesmen would then describe, in glowing terms, a more expensive television set which just happened to be perfectly adjusted and showing a beautifully clear picture. The Consumer Protection Division ultimately stopped this unlawful practice.

Misleading Price Advertising. In the absence of government controls, businesses may charge any price for their products. Similarly, the constitutional right of free speech means that businesses may advertise the prices they charge so long as the prices quoted are not deceptive. In order not to be deceptive, however, a business must intend to sell at the price advertised.

Some businesses attempt to hide their real intentions by false claims to shoppers that "we sold the last one just an hour ago" or some similar excuse. To carry out the scheme, a seller will stock a very small quantity of the advertised product so that the advertisement will not be totally false. Then when the first few customers exhaust the supply, the business can sell more expensive (or more profitable) products to the remaining customers. The law now requires a business to stock a quantity sufficient to meet "reasonable expectable public demand" for the product advertised.

Another type of unlawful price advertising relates to "comparable value" claims. Typically, a business will advertise a product at a certain price ($100), claiming that the advertised product is a "$200 comparable value." The claim means that if you purchased a similar product at another store, the price would be equal to the amount stated as the "comparable value." For this type of advertising to be legal, there must actually be a product *of similar quality* which sells in the same "market area" for the amount shown as the comparable value.

An example of this practice was a sewing machine distributor who advertised through store displays and direct mailouts that his sewing machines—which sold for approximately $100—had a "comparable value" of $295. A state lawsuit alleged that the particular sewing machine sold by the distributor had a true market value of $100 and that no distributors in Texas sold the machine for $295. The law requires a comparable value claim to be based on fact.

"Going Out of Business" Sales. When businesses go out of business, the goods on hand often are sold at substantially reduced prices so they may be disposed of as quickly as possible. For this reason, we naturally expect good bargains at "Going Out of Business Sales." Unfortunately, some entrepreneurs have seized on these expectations by falsely advertising that they are going out of business. Through such advertising, the businesses can attract customers who are eager to take advantage of the expected low prices.

Of course, the "bargain prices" on the merchandise sold at fraudulent going out of business sales generally are not bargains at all. One example of this practice was in a lawsuit filed against a furniture store in South Texas. The Consumer Protection Division's suspicions were raised when the company advertised that it was going out of business in December 1976. Then in January 1977 the same company held a "Grand Opening" sale.

There are several ways to avoid becoming the victim of a fraudulent "Going Out of Business" sale. Several cities in Texas have an ordinance similar to that of the City of Houston, which requires a business to obtain a permit to advertise a Going Out of Business sale. Therefore, by checking with the city clerk, you may easily determine whether a business has properly registered to conduct such a sale.

Comparison shopping is the second (and most reliable) self-protection tool. If you intend to buy a particular item at a Going Out of Business sale, compare the price normally charged for that item.

Misrepresentation

Misrepresentation is identical, in legal terms, to false advertising. The only difference between the two is the means by which the unlawful act is practiced. False advertising, like all advertising, is aimed at the public generally or at certain identifiable segments of the public—such as teenagers, recreation buffs, or homeowners. Misrepresentation, on the other hand, is practiced on an individual basis—normally by a salesman in direct, face-to-face contact with the potential victim. In either case, the purpose is the same: to convince us that some claim about the product, service, business or salesperson is true when it is not.

Misrepresentation may be divided into two categories: that which relates to the product or service, and that which relates to the business or salesperson.

Misrepresentation About the Product or Service

Most misrepresentations are false claims about a product or service. The intention behind such misrepresentations is to convince us that something is a better buy than it actually is. The following specific types of product or service misrepresentations illustrate that misrepresentations of this sort are not limited to any particular transaction.

1. Quality, Benefits, Quantity. False representations relating to the quality of goods, the benefits to be derived from the purchase of goods or services, or the quantity of a particular product or service which will be delivered are illegal.

Beginning in 1976, a rash of "overseas employment" agencies opened in Texas. By misrepresenting the benefits of their services, these businesses were able to swindle hundreds of thousands of dollars from Texas consumers. Salespersons claimed that for a fee of $395, consumers could obtain employment in the skilled trades on the trans-Alaska pipeline. The Consumer Protection Division filed suit against several companies after discovering that no consumers had obtained jobs. The investigation revealed that only Alaskan residents who were members of local unions could work on the advertised jobs.

2. Geographic Origin. Many of us have a preference for goods which are manufactured or produced in a particular locale. For example, until recently, there was a strong buyer preference for French wines and Swiss watches. Sewing machines made in Japan are often claimed to be superior to machines made in Taiwan. The list is endless. Because we prefer to buy some goods manufactured in a particular place, the law requires that representations about the geographic origin of products be true.

For instance, a nationwide cigar company used the name "Havana Smokers" on cigars made of *domestic* tobacco in the United States. A federal court refused to allow the company to use the name even though the company had qualifying language on the cigar labels to show that the cigars were made with tobacco grown in the United States.

3. Need for Repairs. Most products are becoming more sophisticated. There was a time when automobile engines were relatively simple to repair. Today, the diagnosis of auto malfunctioning and the repair of automobile engines are nearly as difficult as the diagnosis and treatment of the human body. Remember the days when a washing machine consisted of a couple of belts (or gears) connected to an electric motor? Today these machines have as many switches, timers, indicator lights, and dials as some airplanes.

There are not too many consumer goods which we can learn to repair in our spare time. Consequently, we have come to rely more and more on the specialized repair skills of others. Most of us have too little technical knowledge to dispute the word of a repairman.

To protect us from those repairmen who would take advantage of our ignorance, the law forbids repairmen to misrepresent the need for repairs. In 1978 seven service stations were prosecuted when it was discovered that their employees were squirting oil on the shock absorbers of customers' cars to make it appear that new shock absorbers were needed. In very dramatic fashion, these employees were misrepresenting the need for repairs.

4. "Original" or "New." Most of us prefer new goods to used. Because of this preference, many businesses represent their goods as new. Once again, the law requires that these representations be true.

An interesting variation of this practice was found in a suit against an automobile dealer. The dealer represented to a consumer that an automobile was a "new" demonstrator when it actually had been involved in a freeway collision. The evidence indicated that as a result of the collision the entire left side of the automobile was damaged to the extent that the front and rear fenders, the left door and the front bumper were replaced. Therefore, the court determined that the automobile was not new.

The example illustrates that the word "new" means "new" in its commonly understood sense. That is, a new automobile is one which is in substantially the same condition as when it left the factory. The fact that "new" repair parts are placed on the product does not transform a "used" (wrecked) product into a new one.

5. Work Actually Done. Misrepresenting the work actually done on a product is similar to misrepresenting the need for repairs. At first glance, it would seem that this type of misrepresentation is simple to guard against. But with many consumer services it is difficult to determine whether repairs have actually been performed.

For instance, a company was convicted of falsely representing to a consumer that his automobile's front end had been aligned. The consumer happened to be a television reporter, and before the car was taken to the shop, the alignment bar was sprayed with a substance that would show fingerprints under an incandescent light. After the automobile was "repaired," an examination with the light proved that none of the alignment parts had been touched.

6. Substitution. We have the right to purchase the products of our choice, and a manufacturer or seller cannot substitute another product for that which we select. The rule against substitution of goods applies whether or not the substituted product is of equal value or quality.

Misrepresentation About the Business or Salesperson

The second classification of misrepresentation relates to the business or salesperson.

1. Affiliations, Sponsorship, Approval. Good businesses and products develop good reputations. A good reputation is so important that it is normally given a dollar value when a business is sold. When a business or salesperson has no reputation, or when the reputation is not good, attempts may be made to associate the business with one that does have a good reputation.

If a business or salesperson claims to be affiliated with, sponsored by, or approved by a particular person or organization, the claim must be true.

This form of misrepresentation is not limited to transactions for goods or services. One debt collector used the business name of "State Credit Control Board" because the collection letters on which the name appeared created in the debtor's mind the false impression that an official government agency was pressing for payment. By misrepresenting the debt collector's "affiliation" with the state, the agency was able to secure an unfair advantage over consumers.

2. Authority of Salespersons. We are all familiar with the negotiation process: one side makes an offer to purchase at a certain price, the other side counters with a different (usually smaller) offer until the parties settle on a mutually agreeable price somewhere between the two initial offers. From a business point of view, "salesmanship" is crucial in this process because the sooner we can be convinced that we cannot do without a product or service, the higher the price we will pay.

One deceptive (and unlawful) practice seeks to disrupt this normal flow of events. The practice is known as "misrepresenting the authority of a salesperson to negotiate the final terms of a consumer transaction." Stated differently, we are led to believe that the salesperson has the authority to negotiate a final price. In truth, he does not. The salesperson convinces us of our need for the product or service; we then "agree" on a price, thus further committing ourselves to buy the product; and then, after we are committed, the salesperson announces that he will have to get the price approved by someone else in the company. Invariably, the salesperson returns after checking with his manager and says that he can only sell the product or service if we pay an additional sum of money. Since we already are committed to the purchase, we reluctantly agree and pay the additional amount.

Although the explanation of how this practice works is complicated, it is surprisingly successful. The practice is unlawful because it unfairly distorts and disrupts the bargaining process. Instead we become committed to the transaction and vulnerable to agreeing to pay the increased price.

To protect yourself, ask specifically about the limits of the salesperson's authority. With this knowledge, you will know to hold back until a final price is approved.

Door-to-Door Sales

Texas has a special law governing your rights and responsibilities when you purchase goods, services, or real estate in a door-to-door sale. This law applies to door-to-door sales occurring after June 11, 1973.

If the following four elements are present, you have the right to *cancel* a door-to-door sale any time prior to midnight of the third business day following the date on which you offer or agree to purchase goods, services, or real estate:

1. You must have offered or agreed to purchase goods, services, or real estate for personal, family, or household purposes.
2. The goods or services must cost more than $25, payable either in installments or cash. If the transaction is for real estate, the purchase price must exceed $100.
3. The seller, or a person acting for the seller, must personally solicit the sale at a residence. Or, in the case of real estate, the solicitation must take place at *your* residence.
4. Your agreement or offer to purchase must be given at the same residence where the personal solicitation occurs.

Disclosure of the Right to Cancel

When you purchase goods, such as housewares, and the purchase price is under $200, the seller must notify you in writing of your right to cancel the sale. This notice must include a statement that the transaction may be cancelled by either refusing delivery of the goods or by returning the goods to the seller within the three-day period. In either case, you are under no obligation to pay the seller anything once the transaction has been cancelled and the goods are in the seller's possession.

If the transaction exceeds $200, the seller must advise you of your right to cancel in three separate ways: first, a notice must be attached to the contract for the sale; second, a separate sheet containing the notice must be provided; and third, you must be advised of the right to cancel the transaction verbally. Each of these notices must be given in the same language as that used in the sales pitch.

Whatever form of notice is required in a particular transaction, it must be given at the time you sign the contract or otherwise agree to buy. If notice is given afterwards, the three-day period does not begin until you receive the notice.

Special Remedies

If you are not told of the right to cancel a door-to-door sale, the transaction is void and the seller cannot enforce the contract. Also, when the transaction is for goods, you may retain possession of the goods until the merchant has refunded any money you may have paid him. You may also sue for any damages that you may have suffered as a result of the seller's failure to tell you of the right to cancel, and if you win the lawsuit, you can force the seller to pay all attorney's fees and court costs.

If you have possession of the goods and decide to cancel a door-to-door sale, you *must* offer to return the goods to the seller and take reasonable care of them while waiting for the seller to pick the goods up.

Unordered Merchandise

Not too many years ago, consumers were flooded with unsolicited goods. We had the choice of either paying for the goods or returning them (sometimes at considerable expense) to the seller. A federal law was enacted which is highly effective in stopping the practice.

Under federal law, if you receive goods in the mail that you have not requested or ordered—that is, unsolicited goods—you may treat the goods as a *gift*. There is no obligation to pay, even if the seller demands it.

Consumer Contracts

For the most part, the preceding sections have discussed those events leading up to the moment that you actually buy a product or service—advertising and representations made in the "sales pitch." This section will describe some important aspects of consumer contract law—the law which applies once we have decided to buy.

A contract is a promise by one person to do something in exchange for a promise by another person to do something in return. Most consumer contracts involve a promise to pay money to a business in exchange for the business' promise to provide us with a product or service. When parties deal at "arms length" and are fully aware of the consequences of their actions, few problems arise. Unfortunately, many consumer contracts involve parties who are not equal, and this inequality is fertile ground for abuse of consumers.

Enforceable Contracts

A contract normally is enforceable if both parties to the transaction receive some benefit from the bargain. When a contract is enforceable, either party can force the other to perform the obligations called for by the contract or pay damages for failing to perform. To illustrate, a contract between you and an appliance dealer that requires you to pay a certain sum of money in exchange for a refrigerator is enforceable because you benefit by getting a new refrigerator and the merchant benefits by getting paid. To be enforceable, a contract does not have to be a good bargain. Although there are clear exceptions to the rule, even if the price you agree to pay is higher than market value, the contract is still enforceable.

Must Contracts Be in Writing? A consumer contract for the purchase of goods or services (*not* real estate) may be enforceable even though the agreement between the parties is purely verbal. A written agreement between a consumer and a business is required only in limited circumstances:

1. For services—when it will take longer than one year to perform the services.
2. For goods—when the price of the goods is $500 or more.
3. Any sale of real estate must be accompanied by an agreement in writing.

What Type of "Writing" is Required? The written agreement does not need to be a *formal* contract. All that is required is something in writing sufficient to indicate that an agreement has been made, which is signed by the parties against whom the agreement will be enforced. To illustrate, assume that you agree to purchase a refrigerator (to be delivered in 30 days) for $500, and the business gives you a signed receipt which says "1 Refrig., 20 cu. feet, all white. $500—Pay on delivery." This writing is sufficient to force the business to deliver the refrigerator as agreed. If there is no writing, you cannot force the business to deliver the refrigerator unless the business has accepted payment.

The same rule works to benefit the business. For instance, assume you sign an agreement with a health studio for a six-month membership costing $500. The agreement says: "6 mos. membership—$500, payable at $100/mo." Assuming there is no fraud or other mitigating circumstances, the health studio could sue you for the agreed membership price.

Is Writing Always Required? Even though a contract for the sale of goods equals or exceeds $500, a writing is not required under the following circumstances:

1. If the seller has begun production of goods that are to be *specially manufactured* and the goods are not suitable for sale to others, such as custom-made upholstery.
2. If the person against whom the contract is to be enforced (the business or consumer) admits in court that a contract for sale was made.

3. If the goods have been paid for by the consumer.
4. If the goods have been received and accepted by the consumer (Partial payment is normally sufficient to make the contract enforceable, at least up to the amount paid.)

Unenforceable Contracts

A contract may be unenforceable—that is, one of the parties to the contract may not force the other to perform—for several reasons; the following are the most common:

1. Unconscionable Contracts. An unconscionable contract cannot be enforced. "Unconscionability" is not easily defined, but it signifies an agreement which takes advantage of someone to a *grossly unfair* degree. For example, if you have no real choice as to where to shop (a senior citizen without transportation, for example) and a store charges you $1200 for a $400 freezer, the contract is unconscionable. Or, if because of a lack of education, language ability, or some other incapacity, a consumer enters into an agreement that gives a grossly unfair advantage to the other party, the contract cannot be enforced.

2. Incapacity to Contract. Some contracts are unenforceable because one of the parties does not have the *capacity* to enter into a binding agreement. For example, a person below the age of 18 may not be held responsible for a contract unless the contract is for "necessaries" such as food, clothing, shelter or medical care. A person who is insane or mentally incompetent generally lacks the capacity to enter into a binding agreement. A person who is intoxicated may not be held responsible for a contract entered into while in a state of intoxication.

3. Mutual Mistake. If *both* parties to a contract are mistaken, at the time they make the agreement, about an important part of the agreement, then the contract cannot be enforced. For example, if you and the business believe that an air conditioner can be operated on 110-volt current (a normal household electric plug) and it later turns out that the air conditioner will only run on 220-volt current, the contract for the air conditioner is not enforceable.

Illegal Contracts

Certain consumer transactions are unlawful, regardless of the time, place, or manner in which they are completed. These transactions are unlawful because the Legislature has determined that the chances of a consumer being satisfied are extremely remote, while the probability of consumer abuse is exceedingly high.

Referral Sales. A referral sales scheme is one which promises you a credit or discount off the purchase price of a product for each potential customer you refer to the company *after* you have purchased the product. The evil of referral sales schemes is that it raises false expectations of benefits to accrue to us in the future from events which are unrelated to the *value* of the goods we purchase. If we believe we will receive a discount because of the referrals we make, we will be more inclined to pay a higher price for goods than we normally would. In far too many referral sales schemes the discount never materializes and the consumer is stuck paying for goods at an inflated price.

A classic "referral sales" case occurred in Virginia when a manufacturer and distributor of above-ground swimming pools promised consumers that if they would allow prospective customers to inspect the swimming pools, a credit of $50 would be applied to the original purchase price for each such customer who purchased a pool from the company. Unfortunately, *every potential customer* referred by customers "failed to qualify" as a purchaser because of bad credit or other reasons. The consumers were stuck with overpriced above-ground pools which could have been purchased from a legitimate business for considerably less.

Pyramid Sales. A pyramid sales scheme has as its object the sale of *positions* in a sales organization, as opposed to the sale of goods. The evil of pyramid sales is that it fails to relate the *ultimate sales* of the company's goods or services to the *number* of sales positions sold; consequently, the potential market is quickly saturated, leaving all chiefs and no indians, all salesmen and no customers.

The name "pyramid" is used because if the sales scheme is diagrammed, it takes the shape of a pyramid. Here's how it works: One or two individuals at the top level of the organization recruit (sell positions) others who buy in at the next level down. These individuals are then told that for each person to whom they sell a position in the organization, they will receive a percentage of the money paid by the new recruit. The new recruits, in turn, also are promised a percentage of the money paid by any new people they bring into the organization. As new people continue to buy in, percentages are paid to each person in the "pyramid" above them. To illustrate, assume that a pyramid scheme starts up its business in a town of 40,000 inhabitants. And, assume that the promoters sell positions to five of the town's citizens. Then, assume that each of these five sell positions to three people. Now there are 15 salespersons. If we assume that these 15 sell positions to three more people each, who, in turn sell to three more people, there are suddenly 135 salespersons, and that number could quickly increase to 405.

In our example five series of sales netted a total of 405 sales persons in a town of 40,000, or one percent of the entire population. After only two more series of sales, the total sales force would exceed eight percent of the entire population. With this many salespeople, the chances of individual salespersons selling any products or services profitably are slim to none. The geometric expansion of the sales force dooms any pyramid sales scheme to failure. Because of this, the sales technique is unlawful.

Chain Letters. Almost all of us have been asked to participate in a chain letter. Essentially, a chain letter is structured the same as a pyramid sales scheme, but the expansion rate is much faster, *and* there are usually no goods or services to be sold by the people who "buy-in."

Chain letters are unlawful both under state law and federal postal regulations. Therefore, as with pyramid and referral sales schemes, anytime you are asked to participate the answer should be a firm "No!".

Delivery of Goods

Once an agreement has been reached between a consumer and a business as to the purchase of goods, the final step in the purchasing process is reached: *delivery of goods.*

When you purchase a product, the business can deliver it to you in one of two ways: They can give the goods to you while you are at the store or send the goods to you at a later time. Regardless of the manner of delivery, the first thing you should do upon receiving the goods is inspect them to be sure that they are the same as those you purchased. If you contracted or agreed to purchase a blue suit, you have the right to demand that a blue suit be delivered.

You have very definite rights as to the delivery of goods. But if you don't exercise these rights properly, you may forfeit them. Remember, however, that businesses also have certain rights during this phase of the transaction. The following sections discuss the respective rights of consumers and businesses when goods are delivered.

Delivery of the Wrong Goods

There are three key terms which you must understand if you are to take advantage of your rights when the wrong goods are delivered: *acceptance, rejection,* and *revocation of acceptance.*

Acceptance of Goods. If the correct goods are delivered, you obviously want to *accept* them. Sometimes, however, you may do something that legally means you have accepted them, even though they may be the wrong goods.

If you do any of the following, the law will presume you accepted the goods delivered, whether or not they are like the goods you ordered:

1. If, after a reasonable opportunity to inspect the goods, you *signify* to the seller that the goods are like the ones you ordered *or* that in spite of the fact that the goods are different, you will take them anyway; or
2. If you say nothing; or
3. If you treat the goods as your own by using them, damaging them, or refusing to allow the seller to reclaim them.

There are no hard and fast rules as to what is required to *signify* acceptance to the seller. One way, however, is to make payments on the goods after they have been delivered. Another means of signifying acceptance is to tell the seller that the goods are "OK." Common sense is the only guide available. If common sense tells you the seller will assume you have accepted the goods if you do or say a certain thing, then that probably will be the result.

Keep in mind that if you accept goods as delivered, the law requires you to pay for the goods at the contract rate. That is, if you agreed to pay $5 a yard for 20 square yards of white carpet, and when the carpet is delivered you "accept" it, you must pay $100 to the seller according to the terms of the contract.

Once goods have been accepted, they can no longer be *rejected*. The only exception is when you accept goods on the reasonable assumption that the seller will correct the situation.

Rejection of Goods. If the wrong goods are delivered, you do not have to keep them. You may *reject* the goods simply by *notifying* the seller within a reasonable time after the goods have been delivered. This notice should be in writing and should state all of the reasons for the rejection.

There are some limitations on your right to reject goods unlike those you purchased. Assume, for instance, that you contract with an appliance dealer for the purchase of a white, frost-free refrigerator, and that your contract calls for delivery of the refrigerator on November 15. If the seller delivers a *blue*, frost-free refrigerator on November 1, the law will allow the seller to *cure* the defect by delivering the correct color refrigerator on or before November 15. The reason for giving the seller the opportunity to cure is that, under the contract, he was not required to deliver *any* refrigerator until November 15. Since, on November 1, he still has over two weeks within which to deliver a refrigerator, the law will treat the first attempted delivery as if it never occurred. If a seller's "time for performance" has not passed, you must allow the seller to cure.

You must also allow a seller to cure an incorrect delivery if the seller has reason to believe the incorrect delivery will be acceptable to you. For example, assume that while shopping for the refrigerator described above, you said to the seller, "I prefer a white refrigerator, but it's not all that important." Then, when the contract was drawn up, "white" was written in the space indicating the color of the refrigerator delivered. If a seller delivered a blue refrigerator, he would have some reason to believe that the color was not all that important to you and that the refrigerator would therefore be accepted. Consequently, if you then decide that only a white refrigerator is acceptable, fairness dictates that the seller be given a reasonable opportunity to cure, by delivering the correct refrigerator.

Once you have rejected goods, you may not exercise ownership over them. If the goods have been delivered before you reject them, you must take reasonable care of the goods and give the seller a reasonable opportunity to reclaim them.

Revocation of Acceptance. Even though you have legally accepted the delivery of the wrong goods, some situations allow you to *revoke* (cancel) your acceptance. If the defect in the goods substantially reduces their value, you can revoke acceptance under either of the following circumstances:

1. Your acceptance was based on the reasonable assumption that the defect in the goods would be cured and it has not been cured; *or*
2. The defect in the goods was not discovered, and because of the difficulty of discovering the defect, you accepted the goods.

Your acceptance must be revoked within a reasonable time after you discover (or should have discovered) the defect *and* before there is any substantial change in the goods. Of course, if the goods are deteriorating or changing because of the defect, you may still revoke acceptance.

If you decide to revoke your acceptance of the goods, *you must notify the seller* of this decision and take reasonable care of the goods until the seller has had an opportunity to reclaim them.

It is important to remember that even if you revoke your acceptance, the seller may still have the right to deliver the correct goods.

Delivery of Broken or Damaged Goods

If broken or damaged goods are delivered, you can either reject them by telling the delivery man to take them back (or by holding the goods and informing the seller to pick them up) or keep the goods and have them repaired, (subject, of course, to the seller's right to cure). If you elect to keep the goods, you can demand that the seller (or shipper, depending on who damaged the goods) pay for the cost of repair, so long as the cost is reasonable.

Delivery of Substituted Goods

Sometimes we purchase goods after examining a model, listening to a description or examining a sample. When you purchase something in this manner, the seller must deliver goods which are like (conform to) the model, description or sample. If they are not, you have the right to reject the goods and either get a refund or demand that the seller deliver goods like those originally shown.

Late Delivery

A bridal gown is of little use after the wedding. So, the time of delivery can be an important factor in deciding where to buy something. Even when goods have a continuing value after the date of delivery has passed, late delivery may mean special problems and expenses. For example, a new washing machine may still be of use to you even though it is delivered three weeks late; but if the old washing machine was disposed of, you have cleaning expenses that otherwise would not have been incurred.

Always insist on a specific delivery date, and once a date is agreed upon, have it stated in writing on the sales contract.

If goods are delivered late, you can refuse to accept delivery and get all your money back, or you can accept the goods and demand that the seller deduct your expenses from the purchase price.

You have a third option in circumstances when goods *must* be delivered on a particular date, such as a bridal gown. In these instances you may *cover*; that is, you may purchase similar goods from another store, and if the goods cost more, the original seller may be held responsible for the difference.

Warranties

Product warranties are one of the most important and difficult problems consumers face. Few consumers understand the legal aspects of warranties; far too many businesses overemphasize the strict letter of the law of warranties, to the confusion and hardship of customers who simply want their goods fixed.

A warranty is a promise. The business promises you that if something is wrong with their product, they will do something about it. The meaning of "something" is what causes all the trouble.

Before attempting a definition of "something," it is important to remember that no law *requires* a business to give a warranty. Even those warranties that are "implied"—that is, warranties written into many consumer transactions by law—may be excluded by selling the goods "as is."

There are two types of warranties: express and implied. *Express* warranties are created by the seller or manufacturer of the goods. *Implied* warranties, unless properly disclaimed, are created by law and automatically accompany the sale of consumer goods.

Express Warranties

Express warranties may arise in a number of ways. First, an express warranty may be created by a spoken promise about goods. If a salesperson says, "This air conditioner will last for two years without any servicing," an express warranty has been created and the product must live up to the claim.

Second, an express warranty may be created by sample, description or model. For example, if you buy carpeting from a sample cut, the carpet which is delivered must be of the same quality as the sample. Or, if a consumer buys (sight unseen) 200 feet of 4-inch aluminum gutters for the roof of his home, the gutters must fit the description and cannot be made of industrial plastic or be only 3½ inches wide. Similarly, goods sold by reference to a model must, upon delivery, conform to the model.

Express warranties may also be in writing. If the warranty is created by a written document, a number of special rules apply because of a recently enacted federal law. All written warranties must be in language that is easy to read and understand. Ordinary words must be used. Also, there is now no difference between a warranty and a guarantee. The terms are often used by merchants interchangeably. Regardless of what it is called, the important thing is what it says.

Written warranties are of two types: full and limited. If you are given a *full warranty,* the new federal law ensures you the following rights:

1. A defective product will be fixed (or replaced) free, including removal and reinstallation if necessary.
2. It will be fixed within a reasonable time after you complain.
3. You will not have to do anything unreasonable to get warranty service (such as ship a piano to the factory).

4. The warranty is good for anyone who owns the product during the warranty period.
5. If the product can't be fixed (or hasn't been after a reasonable number of tries), you get your choice of a new one or your money back.

Although you are entitled to all of these rights with a full warranty, the law does not require that the warranty apply to the whole product. It may cover only a part of the product, such as only the electric motor of a vacuum cleaner.

A *limited warranty,* simply, is any written warranty that is not a full warranty. The term means exactly what it says: something is left out, your protection under the warranty is *limited.* A limited warranty may only cover the cost of parts and not labor; it may require that you return the product, expenses paid, to the factory; it may cover only the first purchaser. When you are given a limited warranty, read it carefully. What you see (on paper) is what you get!

Finally, a product may have both a full and a limited warranty. That is, the picture tube of a television set may be fully warranted with the remainder of the set covered by a limited warranty only.

Implied Warranties

An implied warranty is automatic in any sale of consumer goods unless the warranty is properly excluded. If a seller wishes to exclude an implied warranty, he must do so *in writing* by stating that there is no warranty at all, that the product is sold "as is." If a seller gives a written warranty, however, he cannot exclude the implied warranties.

The most common implied warranty is the "warranty of merchantability." This warranty says, is essence, that a consumer product must be fit for the ordinary purposes for which it is used. Vacuum cleaners must vacuum; irons must iron; automobiles must drive.

A less common type of implied warranty is the "warranty of fitness for a particular purpose." This warranty is not created unless you rely on the expertise of the seller in purchasing a product *and* the seller has reason to know of your reliance. For example, if you ask a shoe salesman for his advice on the type of boots you should purchase for hiking, and the shoe salesman gives the advice, a warranty that the boots will be fit for hiking is created.

Misrepresentation of Warranties

Texas law prohibits a person from misrepresenting the rights or remedies which a warranty creates. For this reason, a seller who explains a warranty to you has a duty to be truthful.

The best practice, of course, is to read fully and carefully any written warranties a seller offers in connection with the sale of goods so you will know exactly how much protection there is in case something goes wrong.

Warranty Claims

When a product fails to meet warranty requirements—that is, when the promise made in the warranty is broken—you must notify the person who gave the warranty (seller or manufacturer) and request that the promises made in the warranty be performed. Your notice should be in writing and should contain the following information:

1. Your name and address and the date;
2. Invoice or purchase receipt number (if this information is not available, the date of purchase);
3. A detailed description of what is wrong with the product;
4. A description of any special harm that may have resulted from the defect in the product; and,
5. A request for appropriate action (depending on the terms of the warranty).

You have a duty to notify the business that the product does not live up to the warranty. Otherwise, the business will never have the opportunity to correct the problem. And notice is essential should it be necessary to file a lawsuit because of a failure to honor the warranty. Because notifying the business is so important, do so in writing, and keep a copy for your files.

When a product is returned to the business for repairs, the law requires that any charge for warranty work be stated separately on the bill. For example, if a warranty only covers parts and not labor, and if non-warranty work must also be done, the labor charge on the warranty work must be stated separately from the charges for the non-warranty work. This requirement prevents a mechanic from tacking extra costs onto a repair bill covered by a warranty.

Automobiles –
A Special Case

Automobiles are the most frequent source of consumer complaints. A national survey conducted by the Office of Consumer Affairs of the Department of Health, Education and Welfare (HEW) concluded that of the 20 most frequent complaints received by state, county and city government consumer offices between 1971 and 1974, automobile complaints ranked first for each of those years. More than *50 percent* of the complaints received by the Texas Attorney General's Consumer Protection Division relate to automobiles. There is no evidence to indicate that automobile complaints are decreasing.

Several reasons explain the disproportionally large number of automobile complaints. First, there are more than 132 million motor vehicles in the United States. The most recent study by the U.S. Bureau of Census determined that 84 percent of all families in the country own one or more motor vehicles.

Another reason for the large number of automobile complaints is that, except for housing, the purchase of an automobile is the largest single investment most consumers make. And in many cases a malfunctioning automobile can result in lost income or additional expenses for alternate transportation, or both. Consequently, when things go wrong with automobiles, we have much more at stake and are more likely to complain to appropriate authorities.

The Consumer Protection Act of 1973 applies to the sale of new and used automobiles, and all the laws discussed in Chapter 1 pertain to automobiles as well, so review them for a complete picture.

New Automobiles

Texas Motor Vehicle Commission

The Texas Legislature recognized that the distribution and sale of new motor vehicles vitally affect the general economy of the state and the interest and welfare of its citizens. On this basis a law was passed creating the Texas Motor Vehicle Commission, the body that guarantees and protects our rights when we purchase a new automobile.

The purposes of the Commission are threefold: First, to ensure a sound system of distributing and selling new motor vehicles through licensing and regulating the manufacturers, distributors and franchised dealers of those vehicles; second, to enforce compliance with manufacturer's warranties; and third, to prevent frauds, unfair practices, discriminations, impositions and other abuses of Texas citizens.

The Commission is composed of six persons, appointed by the Governor, who serve staggered terms of six years each. The commissioners have the power to make rules concerning the manner in which new automobiles are sold.

Licensing. Any person who wants to sell new automobiles must obtain a license from the Commission. The purpose of licensing is to control the quality of the people who engage in the new car business. For instance, the Commission has the power to deny a license to any person who willfully fails to obey the laws relating to new car sales, or who willfully defrauds any retail buyer of a new car. The licensing requirement provides protection to consumers by attempting to ensure that only honest, responsible individuals become new car dealers.

False Advertising. The Commission prohibits false advertising. Although false advertising here means essentially the same thing as described in Chapter 1, it applies to "any form of public notice or statement, however disseminated or utilized." This expanded definition of advertising means that posters, brochures and showroom displays must be just as truthful as radio, television or newspaper advertisements.

Bait Advertising. As discussed in Chapter 1, bait advertising is an alluring but insincere (and illegal) offer to sell a product. Its primary purpose is to obtain leads to people interested in buying a particular type of merchandise and to switch consumers from buying the advertised product to a more expensive or more profitable product. The Commission prohibits this.

Availability of Vehicles. When a dealer advertises a specific vehicle for sale, that vehicle must be in that dealer's possession.

Sometimes unethical dealers will place an advertisement showing a specific automobile, with a price that seems too good to be true. When you respond to the advertisement, you discover that the dealer never had the automobile pictured in the advertisement. You then find the dealer attempting to sell you another vehicle, proclaiming that it's just as good a deal. The insincere advertisement has succeeded in its purpose, for now you are in the dealer's showroom and are "ripe" for a personal sales pitch by one of the salespersons.

This type of advertising is wrong because it solicits your interest under false pretenses and unfairly attracts you away from legitimate businesses.

Untrue Claims. Some claims in advertising simply are not true, never have been true and never will be true. The Commission's rules have identified and outlawed the more commonly used forms of these statements. Any time you see one of the following claims, the dealer is breaking the law, and you should avoid doing business with him:

- Write Your Own Deal
- Name Your Own Price
- Name Your Own Monthly Payments
- Everybody Financed
- No Credit Rejected
- We Finance Anyone

There are other statements sometimes made in advertisements that must be literally true if used. For instance, if a dealer says that no other dealer grants greater allowances for trade-ins, then that dealer must, without qualification, give the highest trade-in allowances. Or, if a dealer says that because of his large sales volume he can purchase vehicles for less than another dealer, then the statement must be literally true.

Finally, a dealer cannot design advertising in such a way as to mislead consumers. The locations of photographs of automobiles must correspond to the location of prices advertised for those automobiles. And, if a qualification is necessary in order to make the advertisement clear, that qualification must be stated.

Manufacturer's Suggested Retail Price. "What is a manufacturer's suggested retail price"? In most cases, it is a figure used as a basis for comparing the local dealer's price for goods. The dealer says, in effect, "See what good prices I have! The manufacturer says I should sell this product for more, but look at this low price!"

An unethical dealer may advertise the manufacturer's suggested retail price while failing to disclose that there are additional charges, over and above the suggested price, which you must pay in order to buy the car.

Now, the law prohibits a dealer from adding any charges to the suggested retail price (if it is used in advertising) *except* the following: (1) destination and dealer preparation charges, (2) state and local taxes, and (3) title and license fees. And, even though these charges may be added, the advertisement must clearly state that these charges are excluded from the advertised price.

A local dealer who is *named* in an advertisement cannot add destination and dealer preparation charges to a manufacturer's suggested retail price listed in that advertisement. The dealer may add only charges for (1) state and local taxes, and (2) license and title fees. Even these extra charges may be added *only* if the advertisement clearly states they are excluded from the price advertised as the manufacturer's suggested retail price.

If an advertisement placed by a manufacturer or a distributor of new automobiles does not name a dealer, then the local dealer may add destination and dealer preparation charges. But these charges, in addition to state and local taxes and license and title fees, may only be added if the advertisement clearly states they are excluded from the advertised price.

Dealer Price Advertising. When a dealer advertises *his own* price, it must include all charges (including destination and dealer preparation charges) you must pay for the vehicle. The only charges which may be added are (1) state and local taxes, and (2) license and title fees.

The advertised price for an automobile *must* be the full cash price. This is true even if the price is qualified by such phrases as "with trade" or "with acceptable trade."

Another common form of automobile price advertising involves the use of phrases like "as low as $1800" or "from $1800." These phrases may not be used in advertising unless automobiles are available at the dealership which are identical to the ones advertised, and at the prices stated. The advertised price must be the selling price of the automobile advertised, and not the unpaid balance after an unspecified down payment or trade-in amount, etc.

Advertising at Cost; Invoice Price. It is unlawful for any dealer to use the term "dealer's cost" in connection with the selling price of automobiles. The reason for this is that a dealer does not know his actual cost on a particular automobile at the time the advertisement is placed. A dealer's sales volume during the year has a direct bearing on his cost per vehicle. Obviously, the total volume of sales during a year cannot be known until the end of the year. Therefore, any advertisement that states a dealer's cost before the end of the year can only be guesswork.

A dealer can advertise a price at a certain amount over "dealer's invoice," since he knows the invoice amount at the time the automobile is delivered. However, the invoice amount on an automobile may bear no real relation to the dealer's actual cost, so the usefulness of such a comparison is questionable.

Trade-in Allowances. Since the amounts of trade-in allowances vary with the condition, model, mileage or age of a buyer's vehicle, the law prohibits a dealer from advertising a specific trade-in amount or range of amounts.

Demonstrators, Executives' and Officials' Vehicles. It is illegal for a dealer to represent a used automobile as new, and it is just as illegal to misrepresent the *type of use* to which a vehicle has been put.

We are all familiar with advertisements offering bargain prices on "demonstrators." The same types of advertisements feature special prices on "executive" and "official" vehicles. The reason these types of vehicles are thought of as good buys is that we consider their use to have been slight. After all, how much wear and tear can an automobile have had if it has only been driven around the block by prospective customers, or if it has only been used to transport executives?

In late 1975 the Consumer Protection Division began to notice an unusually large number of automobiles being advertised in a certain city and sold as "Executive" automobiles. After a brief investigation, the so-called "executive" automobiles were discovered to be former rental cars which had been rotated out of car rental fleets.

The Division put a stop to the practice because it felt that the public's concept of an "executive" automobile was quite different from its concept of a rental car.

The same type of problem frequently arises over the use of the term "demonstrator." Most people think of a demonstrator as an automobile used by a dealer to *demonstrate* the performance of a particular model. In spite of this generally accepted meaning of the term, some dealerships were labeling as *demonstrators* automobiles that had been taken from inventory for the *personal* use of dealership employees. These cars were used in all the same ways other cars are used by consumers. And yet, after a period of a few months, the automobiles would be taken back from the dealership employees and sold to the public as "demonstrators."

To avoid confusion as to what constitutes a demonstrator, an executive automobile, and an official vehicle, the Motor Vehicle Commission made a rule defining the terms:

> "Demonstrator" shall be understood to refer to a vehicle which has never been sold to a member of the public. This term shall include vehicles used by new vehicle dealers or their personnel for demonstrating performance ability, but not vehicles purchased or leased by such dealers or their personnel and used as their personal vehicles. "Executive" and "Official" vehicles, when so advertised, shall have been used exclusively by executives of the dealer's franchising manufacturer or distributor, or by an executive of the franchised dealership. These vehicles, so advertised, shall not have been sold or leased to a member of the public prior to the appearance of the advertisement.

Free Offers; Trade-in Offers. A dealer cannot tell you that any equipment, accessory or other merchandise is free if the automobile can be purchased for a lower price without it. In other words, free must be free.

Similarly, if there are any conditions attached to the "free" offer, they must be described immediately adjacent to the term "free." If, for instance, a dealership offers a full tank of gasoline *free* to any purchaser of an automobile with a vinyl top, a correct advertisement of this offer would be: "Free with the purchase of a vinyl top model."

The Commission's rules also require dealers to live up to their promises on trade-in offers. Frequently, a dealer's salesperson will try to promote sales by leaving a card on a customer's windshield which reads, "Would you take $XX for your vehicle?" If a dealer uses this tactic, he must pay the amount stated on the card, no questions asked.

Automobile Warranties and Contracts

In addition to the specific rules discussed in previous sections, the general law of warranties and contracts discussed in Chapter 1 applies to the sale of new automobiles, so review the main points in that chapter before you purchase a new automobile.

Warranty Complaints

The Texas Motor Vehicle Commission can assist you if you have a warranty complaint about a new automobile. To take advantage of this assistance, you must follow a very specific procedure.

First, when you discover a defect in a new vehicle which is covered by the warranty, you *must* send a letter to the dealer by certified mail in which the defect is described fully. The letter should follow a format similar to this:

```
                              April 14, 1980
ABC Auto Dealer

100 First St.

Austin, Texas 78701


Dear

     On January 1, 1980, I purchased from you a 1980

Ford Stationwagon, Vehicle Identification No. QM12345N54321.
```

My automobile is still within the warranty period in that I have driven it only 7,456 miles.

On April 1, 1980, I observed, for the first time, a dark blue smoke coming from my exhaust.

On April 10, 1980, I took my automobile to your repair shop to have the problem corrected. I picked up the automobile that afternoon and was assured that the problem was corrected.

This morning, the smoke has appeared again. Therefore, it would appear that the problem was not corrected.

In order to protect my rights under the Texas Motor Vehicle Code, I am now giving you written notice of my complaint and am requesting that you repair the defect within the next thirty days.

Thank you for your attention to this complaint.

Sincerely,

When the dealer has had 30 days to respond to your complaint, and has failed to correct the problem, you must then send a *second* letter to the dealer, by certified mail, in which the defect is set forth again. Copies of this letter should be sent to the applicable manufacturer or distributor *and* the Motor Vehicle Commission. Once the Commission receives your second letter, it may hold a hearing to determine if the dealer has violated any provisions of the Motor Vehicle Code. The second letter to the dealer should look something like this:

                                                    May 15, 1980

ABC Auto Dealer

100 First St.

Austin, Texas 78701

Dear

    On April 14, 1980, I sent you a letter by certified mail in which I told you of a problem I was having with my 1980 Ford Stationwagon, Vehicle Identification No. QM12345N54321. Specifically, I told you in that letter that dark blue smoke was coming from my exhaust.

    You have now had 30 days in which to repair my automobile and have failed to do so. Therefore, I am again asking you to repair my automobile immediately.

    If you fail to repair my automobile immediately, I will request a hearing before the Texas Motor Vehicle Commission so it may determine whether you have violated any provisions of the Texas Motor Vehicle Code.

    Your prompt attention to my complaint will be appreciated.

                                                    Sincerely,

cc: Texas Motor Vehicle Commission

Used Automobiles

Used automobile sales have increased steadily in recent years primarily because of the higher prices of new cars. Even though the cost of automobile repairs also has increased, more and more consumers are turning to used car lots to satisfy their transportation needs, finding it more economical to restore last year's models than contend with this year's prices.

Unlike new automobiles, which are sold principally through licensed dealerships, used automobiles may be sold by anyone. The focus of this section will be on specific laws and shopping suggestions that protect you when buying a used automobile.

Odometer Rollbacks

The odometer of a motor vehicle is a device, usually located in the speedometer assembly, that indicates the number of miles a vehicle has been driven. Clearly, the number of miles on a particular vehicle is directly related to the value of that vehicle.

Because of the importance of the odometer reading in determining the value of a used automobile, two separate statutes have been enacted to ensure that the reading is accurate and that no one has tampered with the odometer.

Texas Law. The law of this state prohibits anyone from tampering with an odometer. Tampering includes resetting, disconnecting or turning back an odometer.

Federal Law. In addition to Texas law, a federal statute offers further protection. This statute requires anyone who sells a new or used automobile to provide the purchaser with an "Odometer Mileage Statement" (Figure 2-1). This piece of paper must attest to the automobile's true mileage reading at the time of sale. If the seller does not know the true mileage, he must declare this on the statement.

If you can prove that you were sold an automobile by someone who violated these requirements or who provided false information on the mileage statement, you can collect three times the amount of actual damages, or $1,500, whichever is greater, as well as attorney's fees and court costs in the lawsuit to collect the damages.

ODOMETER MILEAGE STATEMENT

(FEDERAL REGULATIONS REQUIRE YOU TO STATE THE ODOMETER MILEAGE UPON TRANSFER OF OWNERSHIP. AN INACCURATE OR UNTRUTHFUL STATEMENT MAY MAKE YOU LIABLE FOR DAMAGES TO YOUR TRANSFEREE, FOR ATTORNEY FEES, AND FOR CIVIL OR CRIMINAL PENALTIES, PURSUANT TO SECTIONS 409, 412, and 413 OF THE MOTOR VEHICLE INFORMATION AND COST SAVINGS ACT OF 1972 (PUB.L.92-513, AS AMENDED BY PUB. L. 94-364)).

I, _____ , STATE THAT THE ODOMETER MILE-
   TRANSFEROR'S NAME-SELLER–PRINT
AGE ON THE VEHICLE
DESCRIBED BELOW NOW READS _____MILES/KILOMETERS.
                               ODOMETER READING

CHECK ONE BOX ONLY:

☐   (1) I HEREBY CERTIFY THAT TO THE BEST OF MY KNOWLEDGE THE ODOMETER READING AS STATED ABOVE REFLECTS THE ACTUAL MILEAGE OF THE VEHICLE DESCRIBED BELOW.

☐   (2) I HEREBY CERTIFY THAT TO THE BEST OF MY KNOWLEDGE THE ODOMETER READING AS STATED ABOVE REFLECTS THE AMOUNT OF MILEAGE IN EX– CESS OF DESIGNED MECHANICAL ODOMETER LIMIT OF 99,999 MILES/KILO– METERS OF THE VEHICLE DESCRIBED BELOW.

☐   (3) I HEREBY CERTIFY THAT TO THE BEST OF MY KNOWLEDGE THE ODOMETER READING AS STATED ABOVE IS NOT THE ACTUAL MILEAGE OF VEHICLE DESCRIBED BELOW AND SHOULD NOT BE RELIED UPON.

MAKE	MODEL	BODY TYPE	STICKER NO.
VEHICLE IDENTIFICATION NO.	YEAR		LICENSE NO.

CHECK ONE BOX ONLY:

☐   (1) I HEREBY CERTIFY THAT THE ODOMETER OF SAID VEHICLE WAS NOT ALTERED, SET BACK OR DISCONNECTED WHILE IN MY POSSESSION, AND I HAVE NO KNOWLEDGE OF ANYONE ELSE DOING SO.

☐   (2) I HEREBY CERTIFY THAT THE ODOMETER WAS ALTERED FOR REPAIR OR REPLACEMENT PURPOSES WHILE IN MY POSSESSION, AND THAT THE MILE– AGE REGISTERED ON THE REPAIRED OR REPLACEMENT ODOMETER WAS IDENTICAL TO THAT BEFORE SUCH SERVICE.

☐   (3) I HEREBY CERTIFY THAT THE REPAIRED OR REPLACEMENT ODOMETER WAS INCAPABLE OF REGISTERING THE SAME MILEAGE, THAT IT WAS RESET TO ZERO, AND THAT THE MILEAGE ON THE ORIGINAL ODOMETER OR THE ODOMETER BEFORE REPAIR WAS _____ MILES/KILOMETERS.

TRANSFEROR'S STREET ADDRESS (SELLER)

CITY   STATE   ZIP CODE

DATE OF STATEMENT   TRANSFEROR'S SIGNATURE (SELLER)
                        X

TRANSFEREE'S NAME (BUYER)

STREET ADDRESS

CITY   STATE   ZIP CODE

RECEIPT OF COPY ACKNOWLEDGED X_____
                          TRANSFEREE'S SIGNATURE–BUYER

Figure 2-1. *Federal law requires the seller of a new or used automobile to provide the purchaser with an Odometer Mileage Statement. The statement verifies the automobile's true mileage reading at the time of sale.*

Figure 2-2. *When you purchase an automobile, a Certificate of Title must be filed with the Texas Highway Department. It shows the make, model, and identification number of the vehicle, the owner's name and address, and the name of anyone who loaned money to the owner for the purchase.*

Title

A *title* to an automobile is a piece of paper filed with the state (Texas Highway Department) and showing, among other things, (1) the make, model and identification number of an automobile; (2) the name and address of the owner; and (3) the name of any lender who has loaned money to the owner to purchase the automobile and who has not yet been repaid (Figure 2-2).

When an automobile is purchased with money obtained by a loan, the lender (usually a bank, credit union or finance company) acquires a *security interest* in the automobile until the loan is repaid. This security interest gives the lender the right to repossess the automobile if loan payments are not made.

Texas is a title state. This means that once the title to an automobile is filed with the Highway Department, the lender who holds a security interest in the automobile can enforce that security interest against any new purchasers of the automobile until the loan is paid off. To illustrate, assume that you obtain a loan from a bank to purchase a new automobile. When you get the title, the bank will be listed as the holder of a security interest. If you then sell the automobile to another person, the bank will be able to repossess the automobile from the new purchaser unless the original loan has been repaid.

It is extremely important to check the title of any automobile you are planning to purchase to determine whether there are any outstanding security interests in the vehicle. If any security interests do exist, make sure that the seller has paid off or will pay off the loan.

To check the title of an automobile, contact the Motor Vehicle Division of the Department of Public Safety in Austin (512-475-7611) and give them the Vehicle Identification Number and license plate number. They can then tell you the name and address of the title owner of the automobile as well as the holder of any outstanding security interests. This simple check could save you considerable expense and trouble.

Suggestions on Self-Defense

In spite of the statutes protecting purchasers of automobiles, the best protection is not the law, but common sense.

Talk to Previous Owners. Every used automobile has a history. The only reliable way to find out how the automobile has performed in the past, and how it has been treated, is to talk to its previous owner. You can get the name and address of the owner from the title on file at the Highway Department.

Have a Mechanic Examine the Car. Although some used automobiles are sold with a limited warranty, most are sold "as is." This means that the dealer will not be responsible for any defects, even though they may have existed at the time of sale. The only way to make sure you are not buying someone else's lemon is to have a mechanic examine the automobile to make sure it is running properly. When purchasing a used automobile, this ounce of prevention will be worth several pounds (or several hundred dollars) of cure.

Automobile Repairs

Many consumers have paid for unnecessary repairs on their automobiles, or for repairs that do not correct the real causes of their automobiles' malfunctions. As an indication of the widespread nature of the problem, the 1975 edition of *St. Mary's Law Journal* reported that of 2,000 automobiles involved in an automotive repair study in Missouri, 35 percent were found to be improperly repaired.

The reasons for some unskilled and incompetent automobile mechanics are varied and complex. One principal reason, however, is that there are only a few states that require minimum standards of performance or training for mechanics.

In addition to unnecessary repairs, deceptive practices are another major cause of consumer abuse in automobile repairs. The following are the most commonly reported deceptive acts.

False Advertising; Bait-and-Switch. In one case the defendant had advertised the following:

Transmission Overhaul—$69.50

Many consumers responded to this advertisement because of the unusually low price. However, testimony revealed that instead of receiving a transmission overhaul in the commonly understood sense, the "overhaul" consisted of the installation of a "seal kit" only, and that for the complete overhaul consumers had to pay much more.

Fraudulent Discounts and Guarantees. Some repair shops offer bogus discounts and guarantees. For instance, a repair shop may advertise "Tune-Up, 50% Off." If just before the advertisement was placed the regular price was increased by 50 percent, then the discount is fraudulent. Similarly, some repair shops purport to offer "Life-time Guarantees" on their work or products. Later, when the so-called guarantee is read, it turns out to be so limited in coverage as to be worthless.

Inaccurate Estimates. In the car repair trade, the deceptive use of inaccurate estimates has been given the name "low-balling." You are low-balled when, after an initial inspection, you are given an acceptably low estimate of, say, $150, on the basis of which you agree to the repairs. When you leave, the engine is torn down and parts are spread all over the floor. Then you are called and advised that instead of the acceptable price of $150, the true costs of repair will be considerably higher, say $450. Of course, if you don't want to pay the extra amount, you can come and pick up the engine—just as it is. To add insult to injury, you may be told that the engine can be reassembled for a nominal charge which is usually equal to the amount of the original estimate. Given this choice, consumers normally accept the higher charges because of their inability to pay another garage to repeat the process. Because of the unfairness of the practice, low-balling is illegal.

Unnecessary Repairs. Today's automobiles are highly complex machines. Few consumers are knowledgeable enough about their automobiles to accurately diagnose mechanical problems or to know if a mechanic has accurately diagnosed them.

To further complicate things, unnecessary repairs are often made in good faith. Because of the complexity of modern automobiles, mechanical repair sometimes is as much an art as a science. Since the defect (difficult to start, for example) may be caused by several different malfunctions (ignition, spark plugs, carburetor, etc.) a mechanic may have to replace or adjust parts on a trial-and-error basis to see what works. Consequently, although unnecessary repair work may be less likely with reputable mechanics, there is no guarantee against it, and such unneccessary repair work does sometimes occur.

Selling Used Parts as New. This practice is perhaps the easiest to detect if you are willing to take the time to examine the parts installed in your automobile. Rebuilt parts are considerably cheaper for the repairmen to purchase than new, and so there is some incentive to substitute the cheaper product. In some cases rebuilt parts are or can be as good as new; in most cases they are not. By examining the parts installed in your automobile, you should be able to detect the difference.

Suggestions for Self-Defense

Although there is no guaranteed way to prevent deception in automobile repairs, following these suggestions will reduce the likelihood of deception considerably:

1. *Get three estimates*—When major repairs are indicated, always obtain more than one estimate before authorizing the repairs. All reputable repair shops will provide estimates for you; if one refuses to do so, scratch that shop off your list.
2. *Put it in writing*—Whenever repairs are needed, get a written estimate of what needs to be done, the approximate cost of the work, the maximum amount you will be expected to pay, and the date the repairs will be completed. Also, tell the repairman, in writing, to obtain your approval before performing any repair work not specifically authorized.
3. *Get written confirmation of work done*—Once the repairs have been completed, obtain a written list of all repair work done and all parts replaced. If practical, it is also a good idea to demand that all replaced parts be given to you. By doing this, should the same problem recur a short time later, the repair shop cannot charge you for the same repairs or parts. (This demand is best made *before* you agree to the repairs. It lets the repair shop know you are checking up, and it does not allow them an excuse for failing to keep the old parts.)

Special Protection For Repairmen

Historically, automobile mechanics and other repairmen have been given special protection to ensure that customers pay them for their work. Briefly stated, when a mechanic repairs an automobile, he has the right to impose a *lien* on the automobile until all charges due him are paid in full. If the charges are not paid, the mechanic may sell the automobile to recover the money owed him by his customer.

Dallas City Code. The City Council of Dallas enacted an ordinance which provides an extra measure of protection for consumers dealing with repair shops within the Dallas city limits.

This ordinance makes every person or company engaged in motor vehicle repairs in Dallas register with the city and obtain a license to do business. Then, if the mechanic or repair shop fails to conduct business properly, the license may be revoked.

The ordinance also requires Dallas mechanics to give an itemized schedule of charges *before* taking in an automobile for repairs. Consumers must also be told where the repair work will be performed (if subcontracted out to other garages) and how long it will take to complete. Additionally, consumers must be given detailed invoices of all work done, and all replaced parts must be returned to consumers. Finally, any warranties given by Dallas mechanics must be in writing and must be disclosed fully to consumers.

Buying a Home

The purchase of a home is a major event in any one's life; in fact, for most people it truly is an emotional experience. The purchase of a home may represent the fulfillment of a dream; a milestone in the growth of a family; or it may signify stability—a permanent place in the community. For many of us, it is all three and more.

In spite of the emotions that often are wrapped up in the purchase of a home, it is important to remember that it is a personal business transaction. With the average price of a new home approaching $50,000, the risks are considerable unless the transaction is approached with caution.

Before you begin the process of selecting a home, realistically balance your needs against your wants. Rarely, if ever, will they coincide. But your decision to purchase a home is a long-term obligation, and should reflect a proper mix of both. Keep in mind that after a relatively short period of time the newness of the house will wear off, as well as your desire to devote all or most of your recreational time to it. If you have an excessive financial obligation to take care of too many wants, you will find that the home you thought would be a source of entertainment and joy will be little more than a burden—a burden that will considerably limit other activities.

As a rule of thumb, the total cost of your new home should not exceed 2-2½ times your total yearly income. If it does, it is likely to produce monthly payments that will consume too much spendable income. Remember that in most cases your monthly payments will increase as local taxes and insurance costs increase. It is wise to have sufficient budgetary flexibility to afford any increases.

Young couples should be particularly careful when determining the amount they can spend on a new home. If both are employed but plan later for one to stay home to raise children, the substantial reduction in income that will occur must be kept in mind.

This chapter is an introduction to the law of home buying. The first sections describe various types of homes and home ownership, and the ways in which that ownership is transferred. Important things to consider when shopping for a home are discussed. Then, the different ways to finance a home are examined, and the legal ritual called "closing" is explained. Finally, a few words of caution are offered as to what to expect after the home is yours.

Shopping for A Home

There are two ways to shop for a home: You can do all of the work yourself, checking the want-ads, driving through areas in which you want to live, and talking to friends; or you can go to a real estate broker. Since most brokers have access to a variety of listings of property currently on the market, you are likely to find what you want faster. The broker is also able to help with the details of home buying such as completing a purchase contract, locating a lender, and other important, but time consuming jobs. Of course, the broker's services cost money. It is important to remember that the real estate broker is the seller's agent. The broker is paid by the seller and receives a commission based on a percentage of the sales price. You should remain in control of the negotiations. Decide how much you can afford to spend on the home and stick by it. Do not let the broker determine a price for you.

One of the main advantages to having a real estate broker involved is his ability to answer questions or find answers to questions for you.

When you are considering purchasing a new home or one that has been built in the last several years, try to get answers to these questions:

1. Who built the house (particularly if it has been previously owned)?
2. What experience did the builder have?

3. How long has the builder lived in the community?
4. How solvent is the builder?
5. What is the reputation of the subcontractor utilized by the builder?
6. What is the builder's reputation for actually repairing defects if such are found in the home *after* a sale in a timely manner?
7. Have there been any recurring problems in homes constructed by the builder? For example, have an inordinate number of the homes developed foundation problems?
8. If the home has been previously owned, have there been any problems with the foundation, the plumbing, the sewer, or any of the mechanical devices in the home?
9. Has there been a problem with foundations in the area? If so, did the builder take extraordinary precautions or use special procedures to eliminate or moderate the problem?
10. Does the area have a history of flooding? If so, how severely and how frequently?
11. Are there any industrial developments planned in the sur-rounding area? Is any area near the house zoned for industrial or commercial use?
12. Has the home ever required repairs due to fire or other disasters? If so, how extensive was the damage, and what repairs were made?

One of the best ways to determine the quality of a house is by visual inspection. *Look* at it. Look at the attic to see how well it is insulated. Check for holes in the roof and for water stains. Walk the foundation looking for cracks. Check the eaves for rotten boards or boards that need painting. Look for cracks that need caulking. Then examine the exterior roof's condition. It is also a good idea to hire an expert to examine the air conditioning and heating systems. Test the appliances that will be sold with the house—use the dishwasher, disposal, washing machine, etc.

Neighbors are another important source of information. Ask them about schools and shopping. Ask about any problems they have had with their homes because the same contractor may have built all the houses on the block.

Many other questions may need to be asked. For instance, the likelihood of increased taxes to support the schools, traffic patterns, adequacy of city or county fire and police departments, and other services. The main point, however, is to ask questions. The time to learn any unpleasant truths is *before* you sign the contract.

Types of Residential Real Estate

Prospective home buyers also should be aware of the many different types of residential housing on the market today. Our traditional image of a home—a house in which one family lives, surrounded by a yard with trees and sidewalks, is rapidly being expanded to include duplexes, condominiums, and even cooperative ownership.

Duplexes

A duplex is a multifamily dwelling with two separate units that share a common wall. Normally, a person buys a duplex in order to rent out one of the sides. The extra income from rentals helps cover the mortgage payments. There also is a tax advantage because you can depreciate the side that is leased.

Of course, a duplex gives the owner less freedom to adapt the home to his life-style. Consideration must be given to the tenant's right to a peaceful home also.

Condominiums

Condominiums are multifamily dwellings, often resembling an apartment house. A person's ownership of a condominium is in two parts. First, you own exclusively the specific part of the structure in which you live. Second, you have access to and responsibility for the common areas of the condominium such as stairways, elevators, pools, walkways, etc. Your responsibility for the common areas is a joint responsibility shared by the other owners.

Because a condominium owner has exclusive rights to only that portion of the structure in which he lives, this type of ownership is often equated to owning air space within the building. That is, a condominium owner generally cannot make any structural modifications. Instead, his exclusive ownership is limited to that which is within the walls, ceiling, and floors of his living space.

Although the condominium form of home ownership dates back to biblical times, it has experienced a recent surge in popularity because:

1. Family size is decreasing, the demand for housing has increased with a correspondingly reduced demand for space.
2. Land values and construction costs are higher.
3. Tastes are changing. There is a greater acceptance of higher density multifamily housing and a growing desire for close-in urban living.

As Table 3-1 indicates, the increase in condominium units available is remarkable.

Table 3-1
Condominium Growth in the United States

Number of Units In 1970	Number of Units In 1975	Simple Annual Rate of Growth
85,000	1,252,000	274.6%

Figures supplied by the Department of Housing and Urban Development (HUD).

If you own a condominium, you alone are responsible for paying taxes, insurance, or loans on time. If you fail to make payments when due, only your portion of the property can be taken to satisfy the debts. However, all condominium owners are responsible for paying depts due for the common areas. To illustrate, if the roof on the building is in need of repair, each owner of a condominium in the building must pay a pro-rata share of the cost. If your share is not paid, then the other owners can sue you to collect it.

In recent years, many states, including Texas, have enacted laws that regulate the organization and sale of condominiums. Texas law requires that a document stating the rules of the condominium be filed with the county clerk of the county in which the condominium is located. These rules include the amounts that each owner must pay toward maintenance and repair of common areas, taxes, and insurance. The rules also spell out the things that an owner can and cannot do with the condominium. For instance, some condominium rules prohibit children or pets. Others prohibit the building of fences or patios. In short, the condominium rules may deprive you of many rights you might otherwise think you have. For this reason, it is essential that you read the rules carefully to ensure that you understand exactly what you are buying.

According to a 1975 study by the Department of Housing and Urban Development (HUD), there are some recurring problems with condominiums.

Ten Significant Problems Among Condominium Owners

1. Developers commit owners to long term (99 year) recreation leases for swimming pools, tennis courts, etc.
2. Low quality construction.
3. Complexity of documents.
4. Displaced tenants when apartment houses are converted to condominiums.
5. Association operating problems including inadequate insurance, lack of competent leadership, unworkable by-laws or organizational structure, and inefficient collection of maintenance fees.
6. Problems of community living (dog lovers vs. dog haters).
7. Misuse of consumer deposits on condominium units.
8. Nonpayment of association dues by developers.
9. Lack of warranties and engineering reports.
10. Sales misrepresentations, including underestimating operating expenses, unrepresentative model units, and incorrect dates of completion.

Source: Department of Housing and Urban Development, 1975.

Condominium ownership may be the best form of home ownership for you, but it is a form that should be approached—as should other home purchases—with a full evaluation of the considerations discussed. The same may be said for another form of property ownership—cooperative or shared ownership.

Cooperative Ownership

This form of residential property ownership means that several persons share the ownership of a large, multi-unit dwelling. Usually, a corporation is formed with each resident owning shares of stock in the corporation. Each resident (shareholder) is then given the right to occupy a specific unit or units. This occupancy right is similar to a tenancy; the corporation is your landlord.

All shareholders of a cooperative housing project are jointly and separately liable for the debts of the corporation. If one owner or shareholder defaults in paying his share of the debts, the others must make it up. This feature distinguishes cooperative housing from condominiums in that when a condominium owner defaults, the mortgagor (creditor) simply forecloses on the individual unit.

There are still other forms of home ownership. But, this discussion should suffice to indicate that the single family dwelling is not the only way to own your own home.

Before discussing real estate contracts, the subjects of *homestead* and *community property* must be defined. These principles apply regardless of the type of property or manner in which it is purchased.

Homestead

In Texas your residence is considered your homestead. The legal effect of this is that no one can take your home away from you, except for three reasons:

1. A failure to pay your mortgage
2. A failure to pay your taxes
3. A failure to pay for loans taken out to improve the property (purchase money improvement loans)

Condemnation of your property by a government agency may result in the loss of your home (because you have no control over it). This subject is discussed in the section "Ways to Lose Your Home."

Community Property

The subject of community property could take volumes to explain; nevertheless, it has a direct bearing on home ownership and an attempt at understanding must be made.

There are two kinds of property in Texas in terms of the ownership rights of the husband and wife—*separate* and *community*. Separate property is that which one of the marriage partners brings into marriage, or that which is given (by gift or inheritance) to one of the spouses during marriage. Everything else acquired during marriage is community.

Community property is jointly owned by husband and wife. They each have an undivided, 50-50 share. When property is separate, only one spouse owns it.

Separate property may be transformed into community property during marriage if income or other community property is used to pay for it, improve it, or keep it going. For example, if before marriage you own a small lot on the lake with a one-room cabin, the lake lot is yours and yours alone, even after you marry. However, if after marriage you and your spouse build a three-bedroom bungalow on the lot and make other improvements using funds accumulated during marriage, the lake lot will probably be transformed from separate to community property and your spouse will now own a share equal to yours.

Community property can only be sold with the consent and participation of both spouses. In the case of real estate, both the husband and wife must sign all documents that encumber the property (improvement loans) or sell the property (contracts and deeds). For instance, if you borrow money to improve your home but your spouse fails to sign the loan papers, your home cannot be foreclosed on even though it was a purchase money improvement loan. Because of this, most lenders require both spouses to sign any documents affecting real estate purchased during marriage.

Real Estate Contracts

All contracts for the sale of real estate must be in writing. Also, they must be signed by "the party to be charged," that is, by the party (seller or buyer) against whom the contract may need to be enforced.

A purchase contract binds the seller to transfer a "marketable title" by deed to the buyer, and it binds the buyer to pay the seller an agreed upon purchase price. Contracts are used for two reasons:

1. The actual transfer of property binds everyone to the agreement.
2. The contract spells out exactly what the buyer and seller want out of the transaction.

Most real estate contracts contain:

1. The names of the parties (buyer and seller).
2. A legal description of the property to be sold, including its address, dimensions, block and lot number, or its survey "calls."
3. The sales price as well as the method of payment (amount down, method of financing, etc.). The contract usually is conditional on the buyer's obtaining the kind of financing specified.
4. The kind of deed the seller will give the buyer.
5. A description of any known encumbrances or liens on the property so the buyer can knowingly agree to buy the property subject to them.
6. A list of any personal property or fixtures that will be sold with the house (appliances, storage sheds, etc.).
7. Any financial adjustments to be made by the buyer and seller at closing (payments for prepaid insurance premiums, taxes, etc.).
8. The time and place of closing.

In addition to these items, a contract should contain a seller's promise to leave the property in good clean condition. Although the practical enforceability of such a clause is doubtful except in extreme cases, it serves to impress upon the seller his duty to keep the house in good repair.

Also, the contract must contain any and all promises that the seller or agent has made concerning the quality of the house. The promises must be written into the contract, otherwise they are not legally valid.

Earnest Money Contracts

Many real estate contracts call for the buyer to pay earnest money at the time the contract is signed. Normally, earnest money is considered part of the cash down payment on the property (the balance of which is paid at closing) and is deposited with an independent third party who holds the money until closing.

The purpose of earnest money is exactly what the name implies: to guarantee the seller that you are sincere, earnest, about the transaction. If the sale fails to go through because of some fault of the buyer, the earnest money is forfeited.

Escrow Agent and Escrow

An escrow agent is an independent third party who is used as a depository of various documents and funds during the home-buying process. When something is placed in escrow it means that it is placed with the escrow agent for safekeeping, not to be touched until the terms of the escrow have been met.

To illustrate, the earnest money is placed in escrow. Although this money is eventually paid to the seller, there are many things that he must accomplish before the funds are rightfully his. By placing the money in the escrow agent's possession, both parties' performance of the terms of the contract is ensured.

Title

The purpose of a real estate sale is to transfer ownership from the seller to the buyer. In real estate transactions, as in other types, the process is called transferring title to the land. The word title means the same as the word ownership. Unlike motor vehicles, however, there is no land ownership document called a "title." Instead, the title to land is determined by examining other documents such as deeds, contracts for sale, wills, or by looking to see who lives on the land and whether ownership may be claimed through some other means.

Because there is no one document that establishes who owns land, extreme care must be taken to ensure that the person selling the land actually has title to it.

Most contracts require the seller to transfer to the buyer a "good and indefeasible" or "marketable" title at closing. Unless the contract says otherwise, a title is marketable if:

1. The seller owns all that he says he owns;
2. The title is not subject to any encumbrances (see Encumbrances—What You Do Not Own);
3. There is no reasonable doubt that the first two conditions are true.

Sales contracts generally allow the seller to transfer less than all of the ownership of land. Buyers are willing to accept less than full ownership because they want what they can buy more than what the seller is unwilling or unable to sell. For instance, many sellers retain (refuse to sell) mineral rights to residential property. Most home buyers are not all that interested in mineral rights, at least in comparison to their interest in owning what is on top of the land. When the seller does hold back some of the ownership of the land being sold, whatever is held back must be spelled out in the contract between the parties.

The seller's title to land must run in an unbroken chain back to the first sale of the land. Since most pieces of real estate have been sold hundreds of times (think about how many people have moved into or away from your neighborhood in the last few years), the job of tracing the changes in ownership of land is a difficult task and usually requires specialized training. In order to ensure that the title transferred from the seller to you is good, most contracts require the seller to provide either an abstract of the title (an actual tracing of the ownership) or title insurance.

Examining the chain of title reveals whether the seller actually owns the land and also shows any defects or limits on the title.

If the seller is unable to provide you with a marketable title, then most contracts give you the right to withdraw from the transaction and get back any money you may have paid.

Types of Deeds

A deed is the document that actually transfers ownership (title) to real estate. Property is deeded from the Grantor (seller) to the Grantee (buyer). Because of the importance of deeds in determining ownership of real estate, it is essential that they be recorded and filed in the county clerk's office.

Three types of deeds in general use in Texas are: the general warranty deed, the special warranty deed and the quitclaim deed.

General Warranty Deed

The general warranty deed provides the buyer with the greatest protection. When a seller gives this type of deed, he promises to pay the buyer damages if anyone ever proves that there is a better title to the property. That is, if you purchase the property from the seller, and later someone proves that they actually own the property, the seller must pay you whatever damages you suffer.

WARRANTY DEED

THE STATE OF TEXAS |
                                            KNOW ALL MEN BY THESE PRESENTS:
COUNTY OF_____| _____

     THAT_____, of the County of_____and the

State of_____, for and in consideration of the sum of

TEN AND NO/100 DOLLARS and other good and valuable

consideration to the undersigned paid by the Grantee herein

named, the receipt of which is hereby acknowledged, have

GRANTED, SOLD and CONVEYED, and by these presents do GRANT,

SELL and CONVEY unto_____, of the County of _____

_____, and the State of_____, all of the

following described real property in _____County,

_____, to-wit:_____

     TO HAVE AND TO HOLD the above described premises,

together with all and singular the rights and appurtenances

thereto in anywise belonging, unto the said Grantee, her

heirs and assigns forever; and we do hereby bind ourselves,

our heirs, executors and administrators to WARRANT AND

FOREVER DEFEND all and singular the said premises unto the

said Grantee, her heirs and assigns against every person

whomsoever lawfully claiming or to claim the same or any

part thereof.

     DATED this the_____.

                                    _____

                                    _____

Figure 3-1. *When a seller gives you a General Warranty Deed, he is promising to pay you damages if anyone ever proves that a better title to the property exists. Of the three types of deeds used in Texas, this type gives you the best protection as a buyer.*

Special Warranty Deed

This type of deed provides less protection for the buyer because the seller is promising only that he will pay damages if someone who claims through him gets the property from you by asserting a better title.

Therefore, even though you are protected from the seller's relatives or others who may claim the seller sold the property to them, you are not protected from those people who may prove ownership through someone other than the seller.

Quitclaim Deed

This type of deed provides the least protection for the buyer. Only in the most unusual circumstances should it be accepted. All the seller promises with a quitclaim deed is that you can have whatever interest— if any—he has in the property. If another person is able to show that he, not the seller, actually owns the property, you have no recourse against the seller.

Figures 3-1, 3-2, and 3-3 illustrate the three types of deeds and how they differ.

Contracts for Sale of Real Estate

At this point, a word of caution should be given regarding another method by which property is sold. In large real estate developments, some property is sold by *contracts for sale.* In this type of transaction, you pay the seller for the property over a period of time. Instead of transferring the deed to you at closing, the seller keeps the deed until the last payment is made. Instead of a mortgage company having the right to foreclose on your property if payments are not made, the seller has the right to declare the contract void and keep the deed.

There are two particularly hazardous features to this method of buying real estate. First, these contracts typically contain a provision that, upon default, allow the seller to keep all payments as well as the deed to the property. With a mortgage company, the property would be sold, the proceeds applied to the balance of your loan, and the excess refunded to you.

Second, if the developer has mortgaged the property that you acquire through a contract for sale, the developer defaults, then you stand

SPECIAL WARRANTY DEED

THE STATE OF TEXAS |
                         KNOW ALL MEN BY THESE PRESENTS:
COUNTY OF_____ |

      THAT_____, of the County of_____and the

State of_____, for and in consideration of the sum of

TEN AND NO/100 DOLLARS and other good and valuable

consideration to the undersigned paid by the Grantees

herein named, the receipt of which is hereby acknowledged,

have GRANTED, SOLD and CONVEYED, and by these presents do

GRANT, SELL and CONVEY unto_____, of the County of

_____, and the State of_____, all of the

following described real property in_____ County,

_____, to-wit:_____

      TO HAVE AND TO HOLD the above described premises,

together with all and singular the rights and appurtenances

thereto in anywise belonging, unto the said Grantees, their

heirs and assigns forever; and we do hereby bind ourselves,

our heirs, executors and administrators to WARRANT AND

FOREVER DEFEND all and singular the said premises unto the

said Grantees, their heirs and assigns against every person

whomsoever lawfully claiming or to claim the same or any

part thereof, by, through or under us, but not otherwise.

      DATED this the_____.

                         _____

                         _____

Figure 3-2. A Special Warranty Deed holds the seller responsible for damages only if someone claims the property through the seller. It does not protect you, the buyer, from those who may prove ownership of the property in some other way.

QUITCLAIM DEED
_____

THE STATE OF TEXAS   ❙
             KNOW ALL MEN BY THESE PRESENTS:
COUNTY OF_____❙
_____

    THAT_____, of the County of_____and the

State of_____, for and in consideration of the sum of

TEN AND NO/100 DOLLARS and other good and valuable

consideration to the undersigned paid by the Grantees

herein named, the receipt of which is hereby acknowledged,

have QUITCLAIMED, and by these presents do QUITCLAIM, unto

_____, of the County of_____, and the State of

_____, all our undivided right, title and interest,

the same being a_____interest, in and to the

following described real property in_____County,

_____, to-wit:_____

_____

    TO HAVE AND TO HOLD all our right, title and interest

in and to the above described property and premises unto

the said Grantees, their heirs and assigns forever, so that

neither of us nor our legal representatives or assigns

shall have, claim or demand any right or title to the

aforesaid property, premises or appurtenances or any part

thereof.

    DATED this the_____.

                           _____

                           _____

Figure 3-3. _A Quitclaim Deed is rarely used because it does not adequately protect the buyer. With this type of deed, the buyer can only claim whatever interest, if any, the seller has in the property._

to lose everything when the mortgage company sells the property to satisfy the developer's debt.

Obviously, the safest way to purchase real estate is by getting a deed from the seller at the time of sale.

Encumbrances—What You Do Not Own

Few people actually own all there is to own when they purchase a home. Frequently, the seller will hold back part of the property—such as the mineral rights—to preserve a valuable investment while making money selling the rest. There are other types of limitations, however, on what you own when you purchase a home. The deed and purchase contract should inform you of easements and deed restrictions. These two limitations on ownership affect future use of the property.

Easements

An easement gives someone the right to use property according to the terms on which the easement originally was granted. For example, utility companies frequently have easements on residential property to enable them to erect poles for power or telephone lines. Similar easements exist for sewage pipes, buried cables, and other things that must cross over several property lines. You cannot deny the person or company who owns the easement the right to use the property. The only way an easement can be removed is through abandonment (the company removes its poles or pipes) or through a voluntary purchase and sale.

Another common type of easement is that which gives a person the right to cross over property in order to get to other property or a road. Easements of this sort are frequently called "easements of necessity" because the easement owner must have the easement in order to use his own property. Again, this type of easement can only be removed by abandonment or purchase.

Deed Restrictions

Deed restrictions are a second, very common method of limiting ownership rights of a purchaser. For example, a deed may restrict the use of the property to single family dwellings, effectively prohibiting you from renting out a garage apartment. Or, deed restrictions may specify the type and height of fences or the distance that permanent structures must be from property lines. Deed restrictions must be fairly uniform throughout a neighborhood. That is, your house cannot be singled out as the only one not allowed to have a fence. And, deed restrictions can be lost if they are not enforced. Because of the serious limitations that deed restrictions can have on your future plans, they should be studied carefully before you agree to buy.

Financing a Home

Most home loans are made by savings and loan institutions. Business is booming: In 1975, savings and loan associations alone originated $55 billion in loans; in 1976, the amount was up to $64.8 billion; and in 1977, nearly $80 billion was loaned. Other sources of credit for purchasing homes include commercial banks, life insurance companies, and mortgage companies.

In looking for the best mortgage to fit your particular financial needs, you may wish to compare the terms of a private conventional loan with a loan insured through the Federal Housing Administration (FHA), the Farmers Home Administration, or guaranteed by the Veterans Administration (VA). FHA, VA, and Farmers Home Administration loans involve ceilings on permissible settlement charges that may be of benefit to you if you qualify.

Another way to save money when purchasing a new home is to assume the mortgage of someone else. An assumption usually saves money in settlement costs if the interest rate on the prior loan is lower than that being asked in the market. Although a higher down payment may be required to assume a mortgage, the savings in lower interest rates over the life of the mortgage may be considerable.

Good Faith Estimates

When you file an application for a loan, the lender must provide a good faith estimate of settlement services charges you will likely incur (see Figure 3-4). If you do not receive the estimate at the time you apply for a loan, the lender has three business days in which to mail it to you.

The good faith estimate enables you to prepare for the costs of closing or settling a real estate transaction. It should be remembered,

		☐ FHA ☐ CONV. INS. ☐ CONV. UNINS.
GOOD FAITH ESTIMATE OF SETTLEMENT COSTS		☐ VA DATE_____
		NAME OF BORROWER
Farm & Home Savings Association		PROPERTY LOCATION

NOTE: This form is furnished to you prior to settlement to give you information about your settlement costs, but is not a commitment to make the loan for which you applied.

The preparer of this form is not responsible for errors or changes in amounts furnished by others. Tax and assessment proration based on the assumption that there are no delinquent taxes on the subject property. This form does not cover all items you will be required to pay in cash at settlement, for example, deposits to escrow for real estate taxes and hazard insurance. You may wish to inquire as to the amounts of such other items you may be required to pay at settlement.

800.	ITEMS PAYABLE IN CONNECTION WITH LOAN.	
801.	Loan Origination fee %	
802.	Loan Discount %	
803.	Appraisal Fee	
804.	Credit Report	
805.	Lender's inspection fee	
806.	Mortgage Insurance application fee	
807.	Assumption/refinancing fee	
900.	ITEMS REQUIRED BY LENDER TO BE PAID IN ADVANCE.	
901.	Interest @ $ / day, maximum days	
902.	Mortgage insurance premium	
903.	Hazard insurance premium	
904.		
905.		
1000.	RESERVES DEPOSITED WITH LENDER FOR:	
1001.	Hazard insurance mo. @ $ /mo.	
1002.	Mortgage insurance mo. @ $ /mo.	
1003.	City property taxes mo. @ $ /mo.	
1004.	County property taxes mo. @ $ /mo.	
1005.	Annual assessments mo. @ $ /mo.	
1006.	mo. @ $ /mo.	
1007.	mo. @ $ /mo.	
1008.	mo. @ $ /mo.	
1100.	TITLE CHARGES:	
1101.	Settlement or closing fee	
1102.	Abstract or title search	
1103.	Title examination	
1104.	Title insurance binder	
1105.	Document preparation	
1106.	Notary fees	
1107.	Attorney's Fees	
	(includes above items No.:)	
1108.	Title insurance	
	(includes above items No.:)	
1109.	Lender's coverage $	
1110.	Owner's coverage $	
1200.	GOVERNMENT RECORDING AND TRANSFER CHARGES	
1201.	Recording fees: Deed $; Mortgage $ Releases $	
1202.	City/county tax/stamps: Deed $; Mortgage $	
1203.	State tax/stamps: Deed $; Mortage $	
1204.		
1300.	ADDITIONAL SETTLEMENT CHARGES	
1301.	Survey	
1302.	Pest inspection	
1303.		
1304.		
1305.		
1400.	**TOTAL ESTIMATED SETTLEMENT CHARGES**	

Figure 3-4. When you apply for a loan to purchase real estate, the lender must provide a Good Faith Estimate of Settlement Costs within three business days. This estimate enables you to prepare for the expense involved in closing a real estate transaction.

however, that these are estimates. They do not guarantee the amount you may have to pay.

Additionally, a lender is not required to estimate the amount for reserves that must be deposited with the lender or for prepaid hazard insurance premiums. No estimates are required because these amounts frequently require information not known to the lender at the time of the loan application. You should discuss these charges with the lender. The amounts can be substantial; therefore, it is better to know about them in advance.

Between Contract and Closing

After you sign a contract to buy a home, but before closing, a number of important things occur such as checking the title and obtaining financing for the purchase. Most contracts give you the right to cancel the deal if you are unable to make the specified financial arrangements.

You should also check court records to ensure that a lawsuit which may affect the property is not pending against the seller. The county clerk's records will reveal whether there are any liens outstanding against the property. The litigation (lawsuit) and lien records normally are checked by the title company or lawyer who examines the title abstract as part of their service.

It is important to remember that for all practical purposes, closing is a ritualistic occasion, not designed or intended for substantive work. By closing, all arrangements for the purchase and sale of the property must be made; otherwise closing is delayed. It is important, to be sure that you have done everything the contract calls for you to do.

Closing or Settlement

The time for actually transferring the deed, signing the documents, and paying the seller is called closing or settlement. Closing is something of a legal ritual growing out of the days when men used to ceremoniously hand over pieces of dirt to signify the passing of land ownership from one to another. All of the work could be (and sometimes is) done through the mail. But, in most cases, a day is selected, all parties and their attorneys gather around a table, and the complicated process of purchasing a home is literally brought to a close.

At closing you will sign papers legally obligating you to pay the mortgage loan financing the purchase of your home. You will probably sign a note that is your promise to repay the loan for the unpaid balance of the purchase price. And, you probably will sign a mortgage or *deed of trust* that pledges your home as security for repayment of the loan.

You should pay particular attention to the deed of trust. This document gives your lender the right to foreclose should you fail to make the payments in a timely manner. Know what the conditions for foreclosure are; if you have questions, ask them.

One of the principal functions of closing is for all parties to settle financially. As the purchaser, you are the only person who is not paid something at closing. The title company is paid for its services; the lender gets your note (promise of payment) as well as some cash; and the seller is paid the purchase price. You will also find yourself paying for things that you may not understand. There are many incidental charges accompanying a real estate closing that must be paid for either by the buyer or seller. So that all parties have a clear understanding of what they are paying for, federal law now requires a thorough explanation of each of the charges. Figure 3-5 is an example of a typical closing costs or settlement statement which illustrates the wide variety of charges that must be borne by the buyer and seller.

Uniform Settlement Statement

The settlement statement shown in Figure 3-5 must be used at all real estate closings. One business day before closing, if you request it, the person conducting the closing must allow you an opportunity to see a Uniform Settlement Statement that shows whatever figures are available at that time for the settlement charges you are required to pay. The law does not require that the statement be complete. In theory this is supposed to give you an opportunity to prepare for closing. In practice, one day may not be enough, but one day is better than none. You should take advantage of your right to see the statement, but you must request it. Of course, at closing you will be given a completed copy of the statement.

At the time you applied for the loan, the lender was required to provide a copy of the Department of Housing and Urban Development's (HUD) publication, "Settlement Costs And You." This booklet

<table>
<tr><td colspan="2">A. U.S. DEPARTMENT OF HOUSING AND URBAN DEVELOPMENT
SETTLEMENT STATEMENT</td><td colspan="2">B. TYPE OF LOAN</td></tr>
</table>

A. U.S. DEPARTMENT OF HOUSING AND URBAN DEVELOPMENT SETTLEMENT STATEMENT	B. TYPE OF LOAN
FARM & HOME SAVINGS ASSOCIATION	1. ☐ FHA 2. ☐ FMHA 3. ☐ CONV. UNIN
	4. ☐ VA 5. ☐ CONV. INS.
	6. FILE NUMBER: 7. LOAN NUMBER:
	8. MORT. INS. CASE NO.:

C. NOTE: This form is furnished to give you a statement of actual settlement costs. Amounts paid to and by the settlement agent are shown. Ite marked "(p.o.c.)" were paid outside the closing; they are shown here for informational purposes and are not included in the totals.

D. NAME OF BORROWER:	E. NAME OF SELLER:	F. NAME OF LENDER: FARM & HOME SAVINGS ASSOCIATIC

G. PROPERTY LOCATION:	H. SETTLEMENT AGENT:	I. SETTLEMENT DATE:
	PLACE OF SETTLEMENT:	

J. SUMMARY OF BORROWER'S TRANSACTION:		K. SUMMARY OF SELLER'S TRANSACTION:	
100. **GROSS AMOUNT DUE FROM BORROWER**		400. **GROSS AMOUNT DUE TO SELLER**	
101. Contract sales price		401. Contract sales price	
102. Personal property		402. Personal property	
103. Settlement charges to borrower (line 1400)		403.	
104.		404.	
105.		405.	
Adjustments for items paid by seller in advance		Adjustments for items paid by seller in advance	
106. City/town taxes to		406. City/town taxes to	
107. County taxes to		407. County taxes to	
108. Assessments to		408. Assessments to	
109.		409.	
110.		410.	
111.		411.	
112.		412.	
120. **GROSS AMOUNT DUE FROM BORROWER**		420. **GROSS AMOUNT DUE TO SELLER**	
200. **AMOUNTS PAID BY OR IN BEHALF OF BORROWER**		500. **REDUCTIONS IN AMOUNT DUE TO SELLER**	
201. Deposit or earnest money		501. Excess deposit (see Instructions)	
202. Principal amount of new loan(s)		502. Settlement charges to seller (line 1400)	
203. Existing loan(s) taken subject to		503. Existing loan(s) taken subject to	
204.		504. Payoff of first mortgage loan	
205.		505. Payoff of second mortgage loan	
206.		506.	
207.		507.	
208.		508.	
209.		509.	
Adjustments for items unpaid by seller		Adjustments for items unpaid by seller	
210. City/town taxes to		510. City/town taxes to	
211. County taxes to		511. County taxes to	
212. Assessments to		512. Assessments to	
213.		513.	
214.		514.	
215.		515.	
216.		516.	
217.		517.	
218.		518.	
219.		519.	
220. **TOTAL PAID BY/FOR BORROWER**		520. **TOTAL REDUCTION AMOUNT DUE SELLER**	
300. **CASH AT SETTLEMENT FROM OR TO BORROWER**		600. **CASH AT SETTLEMENT TO OR FROM SELLER**	
301. Gross amount due from borrower (line 120)		601. Gross amount due to seller (line 420)	
302. Less amounts paid by/for borrower (line 220)	( )	602. Less reduction amount due seller (line 520)	(
303. **CASH (☐ FROM) (☐ TO) BORROWER**		603. **CASH (☐ TO) (☐ FROM) SELLER**	

Figure 3-5. Federal law requires that a Uniform Settlement Statement be used at all real estate closings. It must clearly explain all costs borne by the buyer and the seller.

L. SETTLEMENT CHARGES	PAID FROM BORROWER'S FUNDS AT SETTLEMENT	PAID FROM SELLER'S FUNDS AT SETTLEMENT
700. **TOTAL SALES/BROKER'S COMMISSION based on price $** @ %		
Division of commission (line 700) as follows:		
701. $ to		
702. $ to		
703. Commission paid at Settlement		
704.		
800. **ITEMS PAYABLE IN CONNECTION WITH LOAN**		
801. Loan Origination Fee %		
802. Loan Discount %		
803. Appraisal Fee to		
804. Credit Report to		
805. Lender's Inspection Fee		
806. Mortgage Insurance Application Fee to		
807. Assumption Fee		
808.		
809.		
810.		
811.		
900. **ITEMS REQUIRED BY LENDER TO BE PAID IN ADVANCE**		
901. Interest from to @ $ /day		
902. Mortgage Insurance Premium for mo. to		
903. Hazard Insurance Premium for yrs. to		
904. yrs. to		
905.		
1000. **RESERVES DEPOSITED WITH LENDER FOR**		
1001. Hazard insurance mo. @ $ /mo.		
1002. Mortgage insurance mo. @ $ /mo.		
1003. City property taxes mo. @ $ /mo.		
1004. County property taxes mo. @ $ /mo.		
1005. Annual assessments mo. @ $ /mo.		
1006. mo. @ $ /mo.		
1007. mo. @ $ /mo.		
1008. mo. @ $ /mo.		
1100. **TITLE CHARGES**		
1101. Settlement or closing fee to		
1102. Abstract or title search to		
1103. Title examination to		
1104. Title insurance binder to		
1105. Document preparation to		
1106. Notary fees to		
1107. Attorney's fees to		
(includes above items No.:)		
1108. Title insurance to		
(includes above items No.:)		
1109. Lender's coverage $		
1110. Owner's coverage $		
1111.		
1112.		
1113.		
1200. **GOVERNMENT RECORDING AND TRANSFER CHARGES**		
1201. Recording fees: Deed $; Mortgage $; Releases $		
1202. City/county tax/stamps: Deed $; Mortgage $		
1203. State tax/stamps: Deed $; Mortgage $		
1204.		
1205.		
1300. **ADDITIONAL SETTLEMENT CHARGES**		
1301. Survey to		
1302. Pest inspection to		
1303.		
1304.		
1305.		
1400. **TOTAL SETTLEMENT CHARGES** (enter on lines 103 and 502, Sections J and K)		

The Undersigned Acknowledges Receipt of This Settlement Statement and Agrees to the Correctness Thereof.

_____   _____
             Buyer   **Seller**

_____   _____
             Buyer   **Seller**

provides an excellent explanation of the various settlement or closing costs that you (or the seller) will be required to pay. It deserves careful reading because the settlement statement contains many charges that need explanation.

Page one of the Uniform Settlement Statement summarizes all costs and adjustments for you and the seller, including total settlement fees and charges found on line 1400 of Section L.

Most of the terms on page one are self-explanatory such as the contract sales price (purchase price asked by seller), charges for personal property included in the transaction, and listings of city, county, or state taxes that are due.

Page two of the Uniform Settlement Statement is likely to be less clear. Therefore, the following definitions should be studied to enable you to understand the statement.

Sales/Broker's Commission (line 700). This is the total dollar amount of sales commission, normally paid by the seller. Fees are usually a percentage of the selling price and are intended to compensate brokers or salespersons for their services. The amount of the commission varies from area to area.

Loan Origination Fee (line 801). This fee covers the lender's administrative costs in processing the loan. Often expressed as a percentage of the loan, the fee will vary among lenders. Generally, the buyer pays the fee unless other arrangements have been made with the seller and written into the sales contract.

Loan Discount Fee (line 802). Often called *points*, a loan discount is a one-time charge used to adjust the yield on the loan to what market conditions demand. It is used to offset limits placed on the amount of interest a lender can charge by state or federal regulations. Each point is equal to one percent of the mortgage amount. For example, if the lender charges you four points on a $30,000 loan, this amounts to a charge of $1,200.

Appraisal Fee (line 803). This fee pays for the lender's appraisal of the property. It enables the lender to have an independent estimate of the property's value. Since your loan is secured by a mortgage on the property you are purchasing, the lender needs to be certain that the value of the property equals or exceeds the amount of the loan.

Lender's Inspection Fee (line 805). This charge covers inspection made by personnel of the lender or an outside inspector. Again, an inspection is necessary to ensure the lender that the property is worth the amount of the loan.

Reserves Deposited with Lenders (line 1000). Reserves (also called *escrow*) are funds held in an account by the lender to assure future payment for such recurring items as real estate taxes and hazard insurance.

You will probably have to pay an initial amount for each of these items to start the reserve account at the time of settlement. Then, a portion of your monthly payments will be added to the reserve account to keep it at a desired level.

Annual Assessments (line 1005). This reserve item covers assessments that may be imposed by subdivisions or municipalities for special improvements (such as sidewalks, sewers, or paving) or fees (such as homeowner's association fees).

Survey (line 1301). The lender or title insurance company may require that a surveyor conduct a property survey to determine the exact location of the house and the lot line, as well as easements and rights of way. This is a protection to the buyer as well. Usually the buyer pays the surveyor's fees, but sometimes this is handled by the seller.

After the Home is Yours

Once settlement is completed and the deed transferred, the home is officially yours. For most people, this is the beginning of many years of enjoyment. For some, however, it is the beginning of trouble. Here are some things that can happen after the home is yours.

Property or Homeowner's Associations

In most new developments a property owner's association is formed to take care of common expenses such as upkeep of the subdivision's pools(s), parks(s), tennis court(s), and streets. Although property owner's associations serve a useful purpose, they can be a source of problems for homeowners.

The first problem encountered by most new subdivisions is not having enough property owners to share in the costs of maintaining the common property. Usually, the developer subsidizes the association until there are a sufficient number of property owners. However, when the developer shirks this responsibility, things can get tight for the association. Higher pro-rata association fees can transform carefully budgeted monthly payments into financial difficulty.

The second problem faced by homeowner's associations usually does not occur until several years have passed and the maintenance fees have escalated considerably. At some point, a property owner will decide not to pay the association fee. Whether it is because the homeowner thinks the fee is too high or whether the homeowner just decides not to pay, most associations will be faced with the problem. The only way to collect is to exercise the rights provided in the deeds. Deeds usually require foreclosure on the delinquent homeowner's property. Most people do not realize that they may someday have to foreclose on the home of a neighbor, and possibly a friend.

Ways to Lose Your Home

The three ways to lose your home are:

1. Failure to make mortgage payments (and other required assessments)
2. Failure to pay taxes
3. Condemnation

You have some control over two of them, but the third is out of your hands.

All governments, federal, state, and local, have the power of *eminent domain*—the power to condemn property for the public good. The power to condemn for certain purposes is based on the general theory that the right of society in having certain basic services must predominate in certain instances over the desires of the individual homeowner. Thus, if a highway is needed by society, your front yard may have to go.

The probability that your home will be taken by the government is not very high. When the total number of homeowners in Texas are considered, a very small percentage lose their homes in this way. Nevertheless, anyone's property can be taken through eminent domain proceedings. Therefore, you should know what to do if it should happen to you.

First, the government may take your property only for a purpose (use) that benefits the public as a whole. The government cannot take more than is absolutely necessary to achieve this benefit. And, it must pay you the fair market value of the property taken. If you can prove that any of these three conditions have not been met by the government, you can contest the taking of your property.

Second, as soon as you receive notice that your property is to be condemned, consult an attorney. The less you delay in hiring an attorney, the better your chances are of preventing your property from being taken.

Renting a Home

The high cost of materials, labor, and land have driven many would-be homeowners into the home rental market. Also, many of us prefer living in rented housing, whether it is because our jobs keep us on the move or because we simply like the convenience of not having to worry about (and pay for) costly maintenance and repairs.

Considering Harris County apartment dwellers alone, the statistics are quite revealing as to the growth of the home rental market. In 1970, Harris County had a total of 134,479 apartment units with an 81.5 percent occupancy level. By 1975, the total number of apartment units had grown to 239,241 with a corresponding occupancy level of 94.9 percent. The number of apartment units has not only increased by more than 50 percent, but the percentage of those apartments actually rented is substantially greater.

How do you shop for an apartment? What are a tenant's rights and responsibilities? What about security deposits? These and other related questions are answered in this chapter.

Shopping for an Apartment

There are several ways to locate a suitable apartment, duplex, or house for rent. The amount of caution you should exercise will depend to a great degree on the manner in which you decide to do your shopping.

No-Fee Agencies

Many listing services will assist you in finding a suitable apartment at no charge. These agencies receive their fees from the landlords who are listed with them. The landlord benefits from the service in that it allows him to spend less time looking for tenants and more time managing. We consumers benefit in that for no fee we frequently find the apartment that suits our needs. The drawback for consumers who use only one such agency is that the choice of housing is limited to the number of landlords listed with the agency.

Fee Required Agencies

The other type of rental listing agency operates by charging a fee to consumers who want to gain access to their special listings of rental property.

In one case, involving a fee-required agency, consumers were charged $30 to have access to its listings of available housing. When customers first called the agency asking if a particular type of housing was available, they invariably were told "yes." Once they paid the fee, however, the listings turned out to be handwritten copies of want-ads that had appeared in the newspaper a few days before. As a result, when consumers checked out the listings, they discovered that the houses had already been rented.

Thus, caution is advised when selecting a rental listing agency. Be certain the service to be rendered will satisfy your particular consumer needs.

Rights and Duties of a Tenant

Any person who rents a dwelling is a tenant of the owner of that dwelling. The owner (or manager) of the rented dwelling is the tenant's landlord. As would be expected, there are certain legal rights and responsibilities that tenants and landlords have. This section explores that legal relationship and points out what a consumer-tenant can expect and demand from a landlord.

The Lease

A lease is a contract for the rental of property (see Figure 4-1). A lease may cover an apartment, duplex, or house. Regardless of the type of rental property involved, the importance of the lease cannot be overemphasized. The basic rights and duties of the landlord and tenant come from this document and this document alone. If the lease forbids pets, there can be no pets. If the lease allows subletting—allows the tenant to rent the property to still another tenant—there is nothing the landlord can do to prevent such an arrangement. In other words, the lease is the law as to the majority of rights and responsibilities between the landlord and tenant.

Unlike the sample lease shown in Figure 4-1, some leases are written in such fine print and confusing language that few tenants can understand them. Many leases are signed, but few are read. If a tenant signs a lease without reading it, he has only himself to blame if the lease turns out to be unsatisfactory. Therefore, the first word of caution must be: *Read before you sign.*

A tenant should never depend on oral statements or promises made by the landlord unless those statements or promises are committed to writing and attached to the lease *before* it is signed. Although you can always take action against someone who deceives you, a landlord cannot be compelled to do anything that is not set forth in writing in the lease. This means that if the landlord promises to repair a defective dishwasher, but the promise is not in writing, you may be able to sue for damages due to the deception, but you will not be able to force the landlord to repair the dishwasher.

Kinds of Tenancy

Several different types of landlord-tenant arrangements concerning the length of time for which the tenant may claim rights to the property are:

1. Tenancy for a Fixed Period. Tenancy for a fixed period is the most common. With this type of tenancy, you are entitled to occupy the rented property for an agreed period of time. The time period may be a certain number of weeks, months, or years. The advantage of such a tenancy is the degree of certainty it provides as to where you will be living for the time period spelled out in the lease. The responsibility of

APARTMENT RENTAL CONTRACT

Date _____

1. BETWEEN RESIDENT(S) _____

_____ and OWNER _____

On Apartment No. _____, at _____

in _____, Texas for use as a private residence only.

2. LEASE TERM. The initial term of the lease shall commence on the _____ day of _____,
19_____, and end the _____ day of _____, 19_____. This contract will be
automatically renewed on a month-to-month basis unless written notice of termination is given by either party at least 30 days before the end
of the above lease term or unless another rental contract is signed by both parties. If commencement of occupancy of the premises is delayed
because of construction or prior resident's holding over, owner shall not be liable to resident for such delay, and the contract shall remain
in force subject to the following conditions: (1) rentals shall be abated on a daily basis during delay, and (2) resident may terminate by giving notice in writing to owner no later than the third day of delay, whereupon resident shall be entitled only to refund of deposit(s). Such
conditions shall not apply to cleaning and repair delays.

3. NOTICE. At least 30 days written notice of intent to vacate must be given to owner's representative prior to move-out at the end of the above
lease term and any renewal or extension period. In the event of automatic renewal or extension of the rental contract, rent shall be paid
through the last day of the month following the expiration of the 30-day notice period, unless owner agrees otherwise in writing. Unless
otherwise specified in paragraph 21, no rent increases shall be allowed before the end of the lease term or any renewal or extension period,
and at least 30-days prior written notice is required of any increase.

4. SECURITY DEPOSIT. Resident agrees that security deposit(s) shall be the total sum of $_____ payable on or before the sign-
ing of this contract. Refunds shall be made in accordance with the attached SECURITY DEPOSIT AGREEMENT which is a part of this
contract. The 30-day written notice provision in the contract will be strictly enforced. If resident moves out prior to the ending date of the
lease term, renewal or extension period, resident shall be subject to paragraphs 16 and 17 hereof.

5. RENT. Resident(s) will pay $_____ per calendar month for rental, payable in advance and without demand at the apartment
manager's office (or at _____) on or before the 1st day of the month without a grace period.
Rent paid after the 1st day of each month shall be deemed as late; and if rent is not paid by the 5th of the month, resident agrees to pay a
late charge of $_____ plus $_____ per day until paid in full. Resident agrees to pay a $10.00 charge for each
returned check. The prorated rental from the date of move-in to the 1st day of the following month is $_____. The above rental
figure is for a _____ furnished _____ unfurnished apartment (check one). Resident's right to possession is expressly contingent on the
prompt payment of rent, and the use of the premises by resident is obtained only on the condition that rent is paid on time. Owner may require
that all rent and other sums due be paid in one monthly check rather than multiple checks.

6. UTILITIES. Owner will furnish the following utilities: _____
Resident shall pay for all other utilities. All utilities shall be used for ordinary household purposes only.

7. THE APARTMENT WILL BE OCCUPIED ONLY BY: (List all adults and minors) _____

_____

8. NO PETS OR SUBLETTING. Residents will not permit a pet, even temporarily, anywhere in the apartment or apartment complex unless
permission is granted in writing by owner's representative. The presence of a pet will subject resident to the penalties, damages, deductions
and termination provisions set forth in the SECURITY DEPOSIT AGREEMENT. Subletting, assignment or securing a replacement will be
allowed only upon written approval and permission of owner.

9. CONDITION OF THE PREMISES ON MOVING IN AND MOVING OUT. When moving out, resident agrees to surrender apartment in the
same condition as when received, reasonable wear excepted. Resident accepted the apartment, fixtures and/or furniture
as is. Resident shall have the right to inspect or inventory the defects or malfunctions within 24 hours after resident is given possession of
the apartment and is given a MOVE-IN INVENTORY AND CONDITION form (for purposes of deposit refund). Resident accepts the premises
subject to and subordinate to any existing or future recorded mortgage, deed of trust, or other lien applicable to the premises or its contents.
Resident shall use reasonable diligence in care of the apartment may not make any alterations of owner's property or fixtures without written consent of owner's representative; no holes or nails in the walls, ceilings, woodwork, or floors; and no waterbeds, antenna
installations, additional phone or TV cable outlets, lock changes or additional locks shall be permitted except by owner's written permission.
Resident will not remove owner's fixtures, furniture, and/or furnishings from the apartment for any purpose. When resident moves in, owner
shall furnish light bulbs of prescribed wattage for apartment sockets; thereafter, light bulbs will be replaced at resident's expense.

10. RULES AND REGULATIONS. Resident, his family, and guests will comply with all written rules and regulations furnished to the resident.
Owner may make reasonable rule changes, if in writing and distributed to all residents. Resident agrees that the conduct of himself, his
family, and guests shall never be disorderly, boisterous, or unlawful; and shall not disturb the rights, comforts, or conveniences of other
persons in the apartment complex. Sidewalks, steps, entrances, halls, walkways, and stairways shall not be obstructed or used for any purpose
other than ingress or egress. Residents shall maintain and clean all patios and other areas which are reserved for resident's private use. Garbage
shall be disposed of only in appropriate receptacles. Swimming pools, storerooms, laundry rooms, and all other facilities are to be used wholly
at the risk of the person using them. Owner reserves the right to control the method, manner, and time of parking in parking spaces and to
control and limit the entry upon the premises by agents, furniture movers, delivery men, solicitors, and/or salesmen who seek to enter upon
the apartment complex.

11. RESIDENT AGREES TO REIMBURSE OWNER PROMPTLY for any loss, property damage, or cost of repairs or service (including plumbing
trouble) caused by negligence or improper use by resident, his agents, family or guests. Residents shall be responsible for damage from windows or doors left open. Such reimbursement is due when owner's representative makes demand. Owner's failure or delay in demanding damage reimbursements, late-payment charges, returned check charges, pet penalties, or other sums due by resident shall not be deemed a waiver;
and owner may demand same at any time, including move-out.

Figure 4-1. *An Apartment Rental Contract is one form of a lease. Like all leases, it outlines the basic rights and duties of the landlord and the tenant. Always read a lease agreement before signing it.*

such a tenancy is that you must continue to pay rent for the duration of the period unless the landlord violates the lease agreement.

2. Tenancy at Will. When you have a tenancy at will agreement with your landlord, it means that either you or your landlord can end the agreement at any time. In Texas, however, advance notice must be given so as to allow the other party to prepare (refer to the section "Notice for Terminating Certain Tenancies").

3. Holdover Tenancy. If you continue to live in the rented house or apartment after the period specified in the written lease has expired, your landlord has a right to evict you. If you are not evicted, then you become a holdover tenant until such time as your landlord tells you to leave or you sign a new lease.

Notice for Terminating Tenancies

Unless the lease agreement says otherwise, when the term of a written lease expires and neither you nor your landlord have given notice of an intention to terminate the tenancy, the lease continues in full force and effect as a month-to-month tenancy. To illustrate, assume that you have a lease for an apartment that is due to expire today. If no notice has been given by either you or the landlord about moving out, the lease will continue in force, automatically renewing itself each month until one of you gives notice.

A month-to-month tenancy can be ended by either party giving 30 days notice to the other. However, if by the terms of the lease the rent is payable every week, or every two weeks, then advance notice that corresponds to that period will be sufficient.

Unless the lease states otherwise, the 30 days notice may be given at a time that does not mark the beginning of a rent-paying period. For example, if you give notice of termination on the fifteenth of the month and rent is due on the first, you will be required to pay rent only up to the fifteenth of the following month. The lease will terminate on that day.

Excluding Tenants from Dwellings

Many landlords have a difficult time collecting rent. Although most of us pay bills when they are due, some people either refuse or are unable to pay promptly. Because a landlord's business depends on his ability to collect rent, there is a legitimate need for efficient ways to encourage reluctant tenants to pay.

One method some landlords use to force tenants to pay rent is to "unplug" their apartments. That is, when a tenant fails to pay rent, the landlord cuts off all utilities. Without electricity, gas, or water, the tenant has little choice but to pay.

If the landlord pays for the utilities, this harsh practice is legally justifiable. However, when the tenant pays the utility bills directly to the utility company, the landlord has no right to interfere in a contractual agreement to which he is not a party.

Another common method formerly used by landlords to force tenants to pay rent was to change the locks so delinquent tenants could not get into their apartments. This would force tenants to go to the landlord, at which time a face-to-face demand for payment could be made. Also, the implicit or stated threat of no money, no key was quite effective to prompt payment. Unfortunately, this practice resulted in more abuse and hardship on tenants than the Texas Legislature could tolerate. Too many tenants spent cold nights on the streets because they were unable to find the landlord.

The law still allows a landlord to change the locks when a tenant's rent is overdue. However, if the locks are changed, the law requires the landlord to leave a written notice on the tenant's door indicating where the tenant may pick up a new key. And, the new key must be available at any hour, day or night. By allowing the landlord to change the locks, the landlord's right to see the tenant face to face is preserved. By requiring that a new key be available for the tenant, the risk of a tenant being forced out onto the streets in the dead of night is eliminated.

The rights to keep the utilities on (when you pay the bills) and a door key available cannot be waived or denied by the terms of a lease agreement. Regardless of what the lease says, these rights remain in force.

Landlord's Lien for Rent

When a tenant fails to pay rent, the landlord has a lien on all property of the tenant that is not exempt and that is found in the tenant's dwelling or stored on the landlord's property. The landlord's lien gives him the right to seize the property and sell it to satisfy delinquent rent payments.

This lien is effective *only* if the landlord's right to seize the tenant's property is spelled out in writing in the lease agreement. It must be underlined or in bold print.

Some property cannot be taken by the landlord under any circumstances, regardless of what the lease states. These items are exempt for one of three reasons: They are considered essential to health or occupation; they are known to be owned by someone other than the tenant; or they are considered to have no reasonable value to anyone other than the tenant.

**Property that Cannot be Seized
by Landlords**

1. Clothing.
2. Tools or books of trade.
3. School books.
4. One car and one truck.
5. Family library, portraits and pictures.
6. One couch, two living room chairs, one dining table and chairs.
7. All beds and bedding.
8. All kitchen furniture and utensils.
9. Food and foodstuffs.
10. Medicine.
11. All property known by the landlord to belong to someone other than the tenant.
12. All property known by the landlord to be purchased on time and not yet paid for.
13. All agricultural implements.

For all practical purposes, the landlord's lien is good only for luxury items such as televisions, radios, and decorative furnishings. Again, the lease cannot take away a tenant's right to keep exempt property even though the rent has not been paid.

Security Deposits

When a landlord rents property to a tenant, there is a risk that the tenant will not take good care of the place. The landlord may have the extra expense of refurbishing the property when the tenant moves out. Since the cost of refurbishing is reflected in higher rent, it is to everyone's advantage to properly care for rented property.

To protect themselves against tenants who abuse property, landlords began collecting security deposits at the time the lease was signed. According to most agreements, the security deposit is refunded if the tenant is current in rent payments and no damage has been done to the property.

Unfortunately, some landlords began to use security deposits as an extra source of revenue, refusing to refund the money under any circumstances. This practice resulted in the enactment of a law that requires the landlord to refund a security deposit if the following conditions are met:

1. No rent is owed;
2. No damage to the rented property has been done by you or your guests;
3. A forwarding address has been left with the landlord; and
4. Advance notice of your intention to move has been given to the landlord.

Figure 4-2 illustrates the form that many security deposit agreements now take.

Your landlord may withhold a portion or all of the security deposit for damages done to the rented property. However, none of the security deposit may be withheld for *normal* wear and tear. For instance, if in a fit of rage over high rent you kick a hole in your front door, the landlord can deduct the cost of the door or its repair from your security deposit. If, however, your carpet has lost its luster after three years of occupancy and normal care, the cost of cleaning the carpet normally cannot be deducted. If any deductions are made for damages, the landlord must provide you with an itemized list of those deductions.

If you fail to leave a forwarding address with your landlord, you still have a right to a refund. However, the landlord's duty to make the refund is suspended until a forwarding address is provided.

There also is a limitation on the landlord's right to withhold your security deposit when you fail to give advance notice that you are moving out. When this situation occurs, your security deposit can be withheld *only* if the landlord's right to withhold it is written in the lease agreement and is underlined or in bold type.

SECURITY DEPOSIT AGREEMENT

(Must Be Attached To Apartment Rental Contract)

Amount Received Toward
Security Deposit(s): $_____ Date_____

This SECURITY AGREEMENT shall govern refunds of all deposit(s), including deposits for any and all purposes, and shall apply to renewals and/or extensions of the APARTMENT RENTAL CONTRACT. The deposit(s) will be refunded only after each and all of the following conditions have been met and after the appropriate deductions, if any, have been made:

CONDITIONS FOR REFUND

1. NOTICE. At least 30 days written notice of intent to vacate must be given to owner's representative prior to the ending date of the lease term, renewal period, or extension period. In the event of automatic renewal or extension of the rental contract, rent shall be paid through the last day of the month following the expiration of the 30-day notice period, unless owner agrees otherwise in writing.

2. FULL TERM. The full term of the rental contract (or any renewal or extension periods) must have ended.

3. RENT PAID. At time of move-out, all rents must be paid in full through the end of the lease term or through the end of the month of any renewal or extension period. Resident may not apply security deposit(s) to rent. Resident agrees that the full monthly rent will be paid on or before the due day of each month, including the last month of occupancy.

4. NO HOLDING OVER. Residents must not stay beyond the date resident is supposed to move out, i.e., beyond the ending date of the lease term, renewal period, or extension period.

5. FORWARDING ADDRESS. A written copy of resident's forwarding address or addresses must be left with owner's representative.

6. CLEANING REQUIREMENTS. The apartment, including furniture and kitchen appliances, must be cleaned thoroughly. MOVE-OUT CLEAN-ING INSTRUCTIONS (if provided) shall be followed.

DEDUCTIONS FROM TOTAL SECURITY DEPOSITS

7. FAILURE TO CLEAN. If resident fails to clean in accordance with the above paragraph, reasonable charges to complete such cleaning shall be deducted, including charges for cleaning carpets, draperies, furniture, walls, etc., soiled beyond reasonable wear.

8. FIXED CLEANING CHARGE. The following charge will be deducted in any event for special cleaning which must be done commercially or by owner's employees: $_____. This is applicable only if owner has a fixed cleaning charge. This charge does not relieve resident from the cleaning provisions of paragraphs 6 and 7 above.

9. OTHER DEDUCTIONS. After inspection by owner's representative, appropriate charges will be deducted for any unpaid sums due under the rental contract, including damages or repairs to the apartment or its contents (beyond reasonable wear); insufficient light bulbs; stickers, scratches, burns, stains, or holes, etc., in walls, doors, floors, draperies, carpets and/or furniture, etc. A charge of $5.00 per unreturned key will be made. Deductions for late payments and returned checks will be as set out in the rental contract.

10. PET CHARGES. Pets are not allowed, even temporarily, without written permission of owner's representative. If a pet is kept on the premises by anyone without prior written permission, a penalty of $10.00 per day will be charged, payable immediately; and in addition, such will be cause for termination by owner of resident's right of occupancy and/or suit for damages. Also, if a pet has been kept on the premises at any time during the resident's term of occupancy by anyone (with or without written permission), a deduction may be made for carpets to be pro-fessionally shampooed and defleaed in order to protect future residents from possible health hazard.

PROCEDURES

11. INSPECTION WITH OWNER'S REPRESENTATIVE. When resident moves out, resident is urged to inspect the apartment with owner's representative during normal business hours, using the MOVE-IN INVENTORY AND CONDITION form.

12. RETURN OF DEPOSIT(S). After all of the above conditions have been complied with by resident and lawful deductions have been made, the balance of the security deposit(s) will be mailed to resident's forwarding address or addresses, along with an itemized accounting of any deductions no later than 30 days after move-out.

13. INSUFFICIENT DEPOSIT(S). If lawful charges, deductions, damages, and other unpaid sums due under the rental contract exceed the total amount of deposits, resident(s) shall pay such excess amount upon written demand mailed to resident(s).

14. FAILURE TO PAY FIRST MONTH'S RENT. If resident fails to pay first month's rent on the first day of the first rental period under the rental contract, resident's deposit(s) will be forfeited and in, addition, owner may terminate resident's right of occupancy and sue for damages, including loss of future rentals, attorneys fees, court costs, and other lawful charges.

15. SPECIAL PROVISIONS REGARDING SECURITY DEPOSITS_____

Resident or Residents   Owner or Owner's Representative

_____   _____

_____

_____   TAA Official State Form 71B, Revised Aug. 1976
                                               Copyright 1976, Texas Apartment Association, Inc.
                                               6225 Hwy. 290 East, Suite 113-B, Austin, Texas 78723

Figure 4-2. This is an example of a Security Deposit Agreement. According to most agreements, the security deposit is refunded if no rent is owed and no damage has been done to the property.

It is important to remember that unless you have a special agreement with the landlord, you may not use the security deposit as the last month's rent. If you use it as the last month's rent, the landlord can sue you for three times that amount of rent plus reasonable attorney's fees.

Move-In Inventory

When you move out of rented property and the question of a security deposit refund comes up, you and your landlord may have difficulty remembering the condition of the property when you moved in. To prevent as much confusion as possible, the Texas Apartment Association (TAA) devised a "Move-In Inventory and Condition Form" (see Figure 4-3). The use of such a form is highly recommended as a protective measure for both you and your landlord. Memories fade; things you thought you would never forget are forgotten. The TAA's form ensures that you and your landlord have the same recollection of the condition of things at the start of your lease.

Pet Deposits

A pet deposit agreement (Figure 4-4) is similar to a security deposit agreement in form and content. The main difference is that while the security deposit agreement protects the landlord against unpaid rent and undue damages to property, the pet deposit agreement protects the landlord against damages to property caused by a tenant's pet or pets.

Because the pet deposit agreement is a contract, you and the landlord can agree to whatever terms you wish. However, once an agreement has been reached, it is binding on both parties. Consequently, if the agreement only allows pets of a certain size or type, you cannot bring in a pet that is larger or of a different type than the agreement permits.

As with all other agreements that you sign, you should read the pet deposit agreement carefully to make sure you understand it *before* you agree to it.

Warranty of Habitability

Until recently, consumers who lived in rented housing could not force landlords to keep the premises in a livable condition. Regardless of

```
                    MOVE-IN INVENTORY AND CONDITION FORM
                             Apartment No.___ _____

           C H E C K - I N                          C H E C K - O U T

ITEMS           CONDITION                                CONDITION

LIVING ROOM
Walls
Ceiling
Floor
Couch
Chairs
Tables
Lamps
DINING ROOM
Walls
Ceiling
Floor
Table
Chairs
KITCHEN
Walls
Ceiling
Floor
Cabinets
Formica-Tile
Range
Refrig.
Vent Hood
HALL
Wall
Ceiling
Floor
BEDROOMS
Walls
Ceiling
Floor
Matt. & Springs
Bed or Frame
Headboard
Dresser
Chest
Night Table
Lamps
BATHS
Walls
Ceiling               form
Floor
Formica-Tile
Cabinets          valid for
Fixtures
Tub Enclosure
CARPET
DRAPES          Taa members
BLINDS
WINDOWS
DOORS               only
LIGHT FIXTURES
SCREENS
OTHER


Check-In Date _____          Check-Out Date _____
```

Figure 4-3. *The Move-In Inventory and Condition Form was created by the Texas Apartment Association (TAA) to protect tenants and landlords. The condition of the property at the time the tenant moves in is put into writing so no one can dispute the facts at a later date.*

PET AGREEMENT
(Becomes a part of TAA Apartment Rental Contract)

PLEASE NOTE: Pets are a serious responsibility and risk for each resident in the apartment. If not properly controlled and cared for, pets can disturb the rights of others and cause damages running into many hundreds of dollars for which residents may be held liable.

1. APT. No. _____   Date of Pet Agreement _____

2. RESIDENT(S) _____

_____

3. CONDITIONAL AUTHORIZATION FOR PET. Residents are hereby authorized to keep a pet, which is described below, on the premises of the above apartment until the TAA Apartment Rental Contract (entered into this date or heretofore) expires. Authorization may be terminated sooner if residents' right of occupancy is lawfully terminated or if the pet rules listed below are violated in any way by residents or residents' family, guests, or invitees.

4. ADDITIONAL MONTHLY RENT. $_____. The total monthly rent as stated in the TAA Apartment Rental Contract shall be increased by the foregoing amount.

5. ADDITIONAL SECURITY DEPOSIT. $_____. The total security deposit as required in the TAA Apartment Rental Contract shall be increased by the foregoing amount. Such additional security deposit shall be considered as a general security deposit for any and all purposes. Refund of the security deposit shall be subject to all of the terms and conditions set forth in the Apartment Rental Contract and the Security Deposit Agreement attached thereto. Owner acknowledges that the following amount has been received toward such additional security deposit: $_____ from the following person _____.
The additional security deposit is not refundable prior to resident's moving from the premises, even if the pet has been removed.

6. NO LIMIT ON LIABILITY. The additional monthly rent and/or additional security deposit under this Pet Agreement is not a limit on residents' liability for property damages, cleaning, deodorization, defleaing, replacements and/or personal injuries as set forth below.

7. MULTIPLE RESIDENTS. Each resident in the apartment shall sign this pet agreement and shall abide by all pet rules. Each resident shall be jointly and severally liable for damages and all other obligations set forth herein, even if such resident does not own the pet.

8. DESCRIPTION OF PET. Only the following described pet is authorized to be kept in residents' apartment. No other pet shall be permitted on the premises by residents or residents' family, guests, or invitees. No substitutions are allowed.

Type:_____ Breed:_____ Color:_____ Weight:_____ Age:_____

City license number:_____ City of license:_____ Date of last rabies shot:_____

Name of pet:_____ Pet housebroken?_____ Name of pet owner:_____

9. LIABILITY FOR DAMAGES, CLEANING, ETC. Residents shall be liable for the entire amount of all damages caused by such pet and all cleaning, defleaing and deodorizing required because of such pet. This applies to carpets, doors, walls, drapes, wallpaper, windows, screens, furniture, appliances and any other part of the apartment or the apartment complex, including landscaping. If such items cannot be satisfactorily cleaned or repaired, residents must pay for complete replacement by owner. Payment for damages, repairs, cleaning, replacements, etc. shall be due immediately upon demand. Residents shall be strictly liable for the entire amount of any injury to the person or property of others, caused by such pet; and resident shall indemnify owner for all costs of litigation, including attorney fees, resulting from such injury.

10. MOVE-OUT. Upon move-out of residents, the carpet ~~form~~ shampooed and defleaed in order to protect future residents from possible health hazards, regardless of how long the pe~~valid for~~ises. Residents shall also be liable for deodorization of the apartment, if such is necessary in the judgment of owner. Such shampooing, defleaing, and/or deodorization will be arranged for by owner and paid for by residents.

11. PET RULES. Residents are responsible for the actions of the pet at ~~TAA members~~ and agree to abide by the following rules:
~~only~~

(a) Residents agree that the pet ~~will not disturb~~ the rights, comforts or conveniences of the other residents in the apartment complex. This applies whether the pet is inside or outside.

(b) Residents shall not permit the pet in swimming pool areas, other apartments, laundry rooms, offices, club rooms or other recreational facilities.

(c) When the pet is outside the apartment, the pet shall be kept on a leash and under residents' supervision at all times. Owner or owner's representative shall have the right to pick up loose pets and/or report them to the proper authorities. Owner may impose reasonable charges for picking up and/or keeping loose pets.

(d) The pet shall not be tied to any fixed object anywhere on the apartment complex, including the patio areas, walkways, stairs, stairwells, parking lots, grassy areas, or any other place within the apartment complex.

(e) Unless owner has designated a particular area of the apartment complex for pet defecation, residents must take the pet off the premises of the apartment complex for that purpose. Residents will not permit the pet to defecate anywhere on the apartment complex, including patio areas, walkways, stairs, stairwells, parking lots, grassy areas, or any other place within the apartment complex. If such should occur, residents will be responsible for the immediate removal of waste. Notwithstanding any provision herein, residents shall comply with local city ordinances regarding pet defecation.

(f) Dogs and cats must be housebroken. All other pets, including birds, must be caged at all times. No pet offspring are allowed.

Figure 4-4. A Pet Agreement is a binding contract between a landlord and a tenant. It protects the landlord from property damage caused by a tenant's pet.

the number of roaches or rats, or how bad the roof leaked, as long as the tenant continued to live in the housing, rent had to be paid.

A recent change in the law now requires landlords to keep rental property in livable condition or face a possible lawsuit for damages by their tenants.

What is livable condition? There is no clear answer. We do know, however, that a landlord cannot allow housing to be unsafe, unsanitary, or otherwise "unfit for living." In other words, a landlord can be held responsible for serious defects in housing.

The most frequent setting in which the landlord will be held responsible for uninhabitable housing is when the landlord decides to sue a tenant for unpaid rent. At the trial, the tenant may now counter the landlord's allegation of unpaid rent by proving that because of the defects the rent is far more than it should be.

Tenants can waive their right to demand that the landlord keep rental property in a livable condition. If your lease says that you take the property "as is"—that you take the property regardless of the condition that it is in—then you cannot later claim that it was the landlord's duty to keep it in good condition.

A decision to not pay rent is a serious decision. If you guess wrong on the extent of the landlord's responsibility, you could face eviction as well as a claim by the landlord that you owe whatever rent remains under your existing lease. Therefore, you should not make this decision without careful thought and provable, good reason.

Ask yourself the questions below. If the answers indicate that you are correct in withholding rent, then do so; but be prepared to face the consequences.

1. Does the defect render the housing unsafe, unsanitary, or otherwise unfit for living?
2. What is the defect? What is its effect on the habitability of the housing?
3. How long has the defect persisted?
4. How old is the structure in which you live?
5. How much rent do you pay?
6. Where is the housing located?
7. Have you *waived* the defects?
8. Have the defects resulted from any malicious, abnormal, or unusual use by you or your guests?

A good way to determine the seriousness of the defect is to find out whether it violates any provision of the city's building code. If so, a court will probably consider the defect serious so long as the answers to the eight questions listed also indicate a serious problem.

Constructive Eviction

Most of us are familiar with the word *eviction*. It means to remove someone from rented property. In law there is a doctrine known as *constructive eviction* which means that the landlord has acted in such a way that *it is just as if* he physically removed the tenant from the housing.

Assume that you live in an apartment where, as part of your lease agreement, all bills are paid by the landlord. One day you come home from work and find that your electricity has been cut off. The apartment is unbearably hot. There are no lights, and you cannot refrigerate or cook food. You demand that the landlord turn your electricity on. He refuses by saying that he wants you to move out. Although the landlord has not actually kicked you out, turning off the electricity has made the apartment so unlivable that you have no choice but to move. If this happens, you have been constructively evicted.

When constructive eviction occurs, a tenant may legally abandon the premises and not be held liable for rent that may remain to be paid under the lease.

A tenant who has met all of his obligations under the rental agreement can claim constructive eviction, however, *only* when all four of the following elements are present:

1. The landlord intends that you no longer live in the premises;
2. The landlord, or someone acting for him, has done something (or failed to do something) which permanently deprives you of the use of the premises without your consent;
3. You completely abandon the premises within a reasonable time after the landlord's act or failure to act; and
4. Your abandonment of the premises is directly related to the landlord's act or failure to act.

If all four of these things have happened, then do not worry about any future rent you may owe. If all four have not happened, proceed with great caution.

Eviction

Eviction means to physically remove a tenant and his belongings from rented property. You are subject to eviction when you fail to pay rent or fail to abide by other provisions of the lease agreement.

Obviously, eviction is a harsh remedy for the landlord to employ. Because of the harshness of the remedy, landlords are required to follow a highly specific procedure to properly evict a tenant. All of the following steps must be performed by a landlord to lawfully evict a tenant.

1. Notice—Unless the lease agreement provides otherwise, a landlord must give you written notice to vacate (leave the premises) three days before a lawsuit to evict is filed.
2. Complaint—Next, the landlord must file a written complaint with the appropriate Justice of the Peace Court. The complaint must be sworn to, state the reason for the eviction, and contain a description of the property (street address, apartment number, city, and county) from which you are to be evicted.
3. Optional bond for possession—If the landlord files a bond in a sufficient amount, the landlord may take possession of the property six days from the day you are served with the eviction suit notice. Without a bond, the landlord must wait until a hearing is held in the Justice of the Peace Court.

   You may prevent a landlord from taking immediate possession by filing a bond that is twice the amount of the landlord's bond. However, you must also agree to pay all costs and reasonable rentals due if the court determines that the landlord's request for eviction should be granted.
4. Filing fee—The landlord must pay the filing fee required by the Justice of the Peace Court in which the eviction lawsuit is filed.
5. Service of process—After properly filing the case, the landlord must request that you be served with a copy of the eviction lawsuit in order to advise you of the date and time the case will be heard.
6. Possession bond—If the landlord files a possession bond, and if you do not voluntarily move out of the dwelling within six days from the date you were served, the landlord may request that the Justice of the Peace issue an order requiring the sheriff or constable to physically evict you and your possessions. This order may be issued before the eviction hearing.

7. Trial—If you do not voluntarily move from the property by the date set for the hearing, you and the landlord must appear in the Justice of the Peace Court to present evidence. If the judge finds in favor of the landlord—that is, if the judge agrees with the landlord that you should be evicted—the landlord must request a "Writ of Restitution" (possession) that allows the constable or sheriff to evict you.

The procedure for eviction is involved and to some degree cumbersome. Nevertheless, when the effect eviction can have on a tenant is considered, the safeguards built into the law against an improper eviction seem justified.

Amount of Rent

Texas does not have rent control. In jurisdictions where rent control laws exist (such as New York City), a landlord cannot raise the rent so long as the same tenant lives on or in the property. In Texas, the only control placed on the amount of rent a landlord can charge is the lease agreement. The amount of rent may be set at any level to which the parties agree.

Most leases provide that with 30 days notice a landlord may raise the rent specified in the lease agreement. These leases then provide that if you are not willing to pay the increased rent, you can move without penalty. Because a provision of this type in a lease agreement lends some uncertainty to a tenant's financial planning, it is always good to look for it and plan accordingly.

Consumer Credit

From 1950 to 1975, the amount of consumer credit outstanding in the U.S. grew more than 900 percent, from $21 billion to $196 billion. This tremendous growth, as well as increased public awareness of how credit works, has resulted in louder public demands for improvement of the system.

What is consumer credit? Generally, consumer credit is all short- and intermediate-term credit obtained to purchase goods and services for personal, family or household use, or to refinance debts incurred for these purposes. It is, in short, "buying on time." Approximately 65 percent of all new cars and 75 percent of all used cars are purchased with credit. About 85 percent of other durable consumer items, such as furniture and appliances, are credit purchases.

For many consumers, understanding how the credit system works is more difficult than understanding which credit practices are unlawful. Because of this, the main purpose of this chapter is to introduce you to the way consumer credit works. After covering the basics of the system, we will cover the special laws that exist to protect you when you use or try to obtain credit.

Types of Credit

The principal divisions of consumer credit are *installment* and *noninstallment* credit; that is, credit scheduled to be repaid in two or more payments and credit to be repaid in one lump sum. Common forms of installment credit are personal loans, automobile loans, home repair loans, and retail charge accounts. Non-installment loans include commercial bank single-payment loans, retail charge accounts payable in 30 days or less, medical or other professional services charges, and public utilities charges.

Within these two divisions are many types of credit designed to meet various consumer needs.

Closed-End Credit

This common form of credit is a loan for a specific amount of money which must be repaid over a set period of time in equal monthly installments. It is the financing method most people use to purchase major items such as automobiles or appliances. The borrower usually receives a book of coupons and returns one coupon with each monthly payment.

When you use this type of credit to purchase a product, you may sign a *conditional sales contract*. The contract is conditional because the actual transfer of ownership depends on whether you make your payments. In other cases, you may borrow money from a lender to purchase a product such as an automobile. The automobile dealer is paid in full from the proceeds of your loan; therefore, your sales contract is not conditional. Instead, the lender will reserve a *security interest* in the automobile so it may be repossessed if you default on your payments.

The four types of installment loans used most frequently in closed-end credit transactions are:

1. Personal Loans. These are cash sums provided directly to the consumer for temporary use. These loans often require *collateral*, that is, tangible, valuable property offered as a pledge of repayment. This form of credit is helpful in times of unforeseen financial emergency.

2. Home Mortgage Loans. Most homes are purchased by using one of the three forms of this type of installment, closed-end credit: the conventional loan, the insurance loan, or the federally-insured loan. Home loans are usually paid over a long period of time, and monthly payments usually include the costs of interest, principal, insurance and taxes.

Conventional loans are usually borrowed from banks, credit unions or savings-and-loan associations. Down payments are a substantial part of the purchase price, and the land and buildings bought frequently serve as collateral. Insurance loans are offered by insurance companies and often require higher down payments and have shorter periods for repayment than other types of home loans. Federally-insured loans (VA and FHA) require no down payments, or lower down payments than other home loans, and allow longer repayment periods. This type of loan offers more advantages to consumers because the government shares part of the risk with the lending institution.

3. Passbook Loans. Loans of this nature involve borrowing against money already held in a savings account. A portion of your account equal to the amount of the loan is "frozen" until the loan is repaid, but you continue earning interest on the account.

4. Consolidation Loans. Some consumers find that their monthly outgo for payments is nearing or exceeding their income. A consolidation loan allows for all individual debts to be repaid, and reduces the *amount* of monthly payments by increasing the *number* of monthly payments. Since there is a charge for this service, the consumer pays more in the end for the accumulated debt.

Open-End Credit

This form of credit enables a borrower to have continuous access to new credit so long as the total balance owed is at or below the agreed upon credit limits. The most common examples of this type of credit are: (1) open accounts, (2) revolving credit, and (3) option charge accounts.

1. Open Accounts. An open account is an arrangement between a creditor (a store) and a consumer permitting purchases with no down payment and no service charge. Such an account offers the convenience of credit buying without finance charges. However, open accounts must be paid in full at the end of each 30-day billing period.

2. Revolving Credit. Revolving credit means that the store sets a limit on the amount you can owe at any one time, based on your income and other expenses. Therefore, you have access to a wide range of goods and services, but you cannot overextend your purchases. There is a charge for this type of credit.

3. Option Charge Accounts. These accounts allow a minimum balance outstanding up to an agreed-upon limit, and the customer has the option each month to pay the bill in full or to pay only a portion of it. Partial payments must be at least a minimum amount, and a service charge is added to the next month's billing.

Service Credit

Although it is not commonly thought of as credit, service credit is of major importance to consumers. It consists of end-of-the-month payments for the use of utilities like telephone, gas and electricity, and monthly payments for the services of professionals such as doctors and dentists.

The Price of Credit

Since Biblical times consumers and businesses have been exhorted to be careful with credit. Deuteronomy, Chapter XV, verses 1-6, offers a rule of thumb for consumer credit: "Every seven years, all debts are to be cleared off the books and all pledges retired."

Unfortunately, many of us do not follow this Biblical admonition, and even fewer of us shop and compare for the best credit costs. Too often, we are concerned only with the relative purchase price of an item and how much we have to pay each month. Since the cost of credit can substantially increase the price of goods and services, you should shop for credit as carefully as you do for the merchandise itself. A good rule of thumb is to limit total credit commitments to no more than 20 percent of your take-home pay after rent or mortgage payments.

There are many costs that add up to the "price of credit." To understand the rights and remedies provided by law, it is necessary to examine each of these costs.

Finance Charge

The total of all charges you pay to obtain credit, including service charges, credit insurance, interest, and filing fees, is called the "finance charge." Federal law requires that creditors inform consumers of this charge in all credit transactions.

Interest

Interest is a percentage of the amount of money borrowed which represents the lender's *direct* charge for the credit extended. Much of the variance in finance charges is due to the different methods of computing interest rates. Federal law now requires creditors to state on the bill the method being used. The three most common methods are:

1. *Adjusted balance method*—This is the best method for consumers. Finance charges are figured on the *unpaid* balance at the end of the billing period.
2. *Previous balance method*—Commonly used by retail stores, this method involves the computation of finance charges on the amount owed on the final date of the previous month. Since it does not take account of payments made after that date or credit due for returned merchandise, it is the least favorable method for consumers. One study determined that this method cost 16 percent more than interest calculated by the adjusted balance method!
3. *Average daily balance method*—This method, commonly used by banks, was also found to be 16 percent more costly than the adjusted balance method. Interest is calculated on the average daily balance during the billing period. Paying promptly will limit the cost of accounts charged on this basis.

Annual Percentage Rate (APR). Federal law requires all creditors to quote the annual percentage rate (APR) of loans to customers. It is the "effective" rate you pay for credit, and it allows you to comparison shop for credit. The other methods of describing interest, the *add-on* method and the *discount* method, reflect only about one-half of the true annual percentage rate of a loan.

When the add-on method is used, the borrower pays interest on the total amount of the loan over a specified period of time, but does not have the use of the amount borrowed over the full period of the loan. (Each monthly payment reduces the amount of the loan the borrower has available to use). On the other hand, the *discount* method deducts the amount of the interest initially from the amount given the borrower. Then, the remaining principal and interest are repaid in monthly installments. The APR is computed by multiplying one twelfth of the annual interest rate *by the amount owed at that time.* Since the law requires that the APR reflect the interest paid on the declining balance rather than on the gross amount of the loan, it allows you to see how much interest you pay on the amount of money actually used during a time period. Because each APR is computed in the same way, you can now compare a loan with an APR of 8 percent to one with an APR of 15 percent and know that the 8 percent loan is cheaper.

Interest Rate Ceilings. Efforts to regulate allowable interest rates go as far back as 2400 B.C., in India, when a 24 percent limit on interest was established. The ancient Greeks and Romans made similar attempts with rate ceilings varying from no interest to 12½ percent. The Christian era introduced a moral issue by making it a sin to "take usury," that is, any payment in excess of what was lent. A strict interpretation of this precept, which lasted for centuries, resulted in black market interest rates of up to 300 percent because no legitimate lender would loan money if he could not charge for the service. The black market flourished because people have always needed credit.

The English had legal interest rates of 6 to 8 percent during the seventeenth and eighteenth centuries. Although the English usury laws were abolished in the mid 1800s, the concept was adopted in the American colonies. Today there are still usury laws in every state except New Hampshire.

Usury laws set a *legal rate*, which is the statutory limit when no interest terms are mentioned between the parties, and a *contract rate*, or maximum that parties to a loan contract may agree upon. The majority of states fix legal rates between 6 and 8 percent and contract rates between 8 and 12 percent. For Texas the legal rate is 6 percent; the contract rate here is 10 percent.

Creditors who violate the usury laws in Texas are liable to their debtors for twice the amount of the interest charged, and if the interest exceeds twice the statutory rate, the creditor also forfeits the principal.

Generally, small loans and installment loans are costly to financial institutions, and exceptions to the usury laws have been carved out to make such loans available to the public. For instance, Texas law allows higher interest rates for installment loans, secondary mortgage loans, retail sales of goods, installment motor vehicle sales, loans for insurance premiums, and pawnbroker fees. In each case, the loan interest rates may exceed 10 percent if the lender complies with certain requirements. It is assumed that the lenders, who must meet state licensure requirements and regulations, will offer interest rates at a reasonable level because of the competition among small loan lenders. Lenders who charge higher than the allowable interest rates for loans in this category are subject to penalties similar to those imposed for violations of the general usury laws.

Credit Insurance

This insurance is sold to persons borrowing money or purchasing goods or services on the installment plan. It pays off the entire balance due if the debtor dies, or it covers missed payments if the debtor becomes disabled. The borrowing customer is the insured; the creditor is the primary beneficiary and is paid directly by the insurance company when the debtor dies or becomes disabled.

When credit insurance was first marketed in the early 1900s creditors paid for it themselves. Today premium costs are usually passed on to consumers. Credit insurance sales account for much of the profit credit institutions earn; one-third to one-half of some creditors' income is derived from such sales! The premium charges added onto most credit transactions are so small that many consumers are not aware of this cost. Federal law, however, mandates that the cost of credit insurance be disclosed to consumers unless its purchase is not required. If it is not required, you must be clearly informed of the fact in writing and must give a dated, signed statement indicating a desire for the insurance. Texas protects consumers in this area by strictly forbidding the sale of credit insurance on loans under $100.

Credit Institutions

Consumer loans are available from a number of sources. The type of source you use depends largely on the type of loan you seek.

Commercial banks charge lower interest rates than some other lending institutions. However, they require a good reason for the loan and a debtor with a good credit record. Banks that are nationally chartered (National or N.A. appear in their names) are regulated by the U.S. Comptroller of the Currency. Those that are state-chartered are regulated by the Banking Department of Texas.

Savings-and-loan associations operate similarly to banks and charge comparable interest rates. Home loans are their primary business, but loans may be made for certain other purposes. Federally chartered savings-and-loan associations are regulated by the Federal Home Loan Bank Board. State-chartered savings and loan associations are regulated by the Texas Savings and Loan Department.

Credit unions require people to join before they can obtain credit. Members borrow at interest rates similar to those charged by banks or savings-and-loan associations. Federally chartered credit unions are under the supervision of the Federal Credit Union Administration. The Texas Credit Union Commission regulates those with state charters.

Personal finance and *small loan companies* charge higher interest rates than other lending institutions because they loan small amounts to "high risk" consumers. Such institutions are licensed and regulated by the Texas Consumer Credit Commissioner.

Establishing Credit

A consumer is considered a "good credit risk" if he or she has a stable job with regular pay, always pays bills when they are due, and owns property worth more than the sum being borrowed. If you have a good credit record, you are able to borrow at lower interest rates—credit costs you less than it does those with poor credit records.

Many young people are in a double bind, a Catch 22: they cannot establish a good credit record because no one will grant them credit, and no one will grant them credit because they have no credit record. Remember, there are no laws *requiring* stores and lending institutions to give charge accounts, credit cards, or loans to any person. If you have no established credit record, you may need a *co-signer* for a loan. A co-signer is a parent or other responsible adult with a good credit record who agrees to pay for the loan if you do not complete your payments. After you have paid off one co-signed note, the lending institution probably will give you a loan the next time on your signature alone.

Another means of establishing credit is to open a savings account and make regular deposits. When you have a substantial amount, you can apply for a loan from the same institution, using your savings account as collateral.

Still another idea for obtaining credit is to trade at a drug store, dry cleaner, or other neighborhood business that you know offers charge accounts. After trading at the same store for several months, apply for your own account; make charges regularly for a few months and always pay your bills promptly. You can then use the business as a reference when applying for other credit.

You should also check with department stores to see if they offer special "limited credit" accounts for young adults. If you build up a good credit record with the store, you can then ask that your credit limit be raised.

When you have established a credit record, you can then apply for a gas company credit card, a bank credit card, and a charge account with a nationwide store chain. After this, as long as you use credit wisely and do not overextend yourself, you should have no difficulty obtaining credit when you need it.

Shopping for a Loan

In addition to considering the "price of credit," you should carefully review the terms of a loan agreement to avoid unnecessary problems. First determine what the required down payment is and whether you can afford the monthly payments. Take care to learn whether the schedule includes a "ballooning" plan whereby the last payment due is much higher than the regular monthly payments. Know what the consequences are if you miss a payment or make a partial payment, and whether there is a grace period. In some loan contracts default may mean repossession of the goods purchased with the loan and may even result in your being forced to pay court costs if a lawsuit is filed to collect the loan. Find out how much of the finance charge will be refunded if the loan is repaid earlier than the payment schedule requires. If the loan involves the pledge of your car, home or other property as security, be aware of the obligations and risks this entails.

Co-Signing Loans—A Word of Caution

If you have an established credit record, it is likely a friend or relative with less credit will ask you to help him obtain a loan by co-signing the loan agreement. According to many loan officers at banks, credit unions, and other financial institutions, co-signers often think that by co-signing they are merely stating their opinion that the borrower is a good credit risk, or endorsing him as being generally trustworthy—something like giving a reference. On the contrary, co-signing a loan agreement legally obligates the co-signer to repay the loan if the debtor defaults.

Some loan officers try to discourage co-signing by pointing out all of the liabilities it can create. In addition to the possibility of having to pay off somebody else's loan, you likely will be reducing your own capacity to borrow by co-signing. If you should later need a loan for an emergency, this might be a problem.

Because of the seriousness of co-signing a loan, keep these things in mind: First, be absolutely sure you can pay off the loan if necessary. (Remember, that means you must be able to meet the monthly loan payments in addition to your other bills or be able to pay the loan off in a lump sum.) If you cannot guarantee all of the loan amount, perhaps you will want to co-sign for only part.

Second, you should know the borrower well and be aware of his financial status, and character. This may mean asking some rather pointed questions and demanding proof of salary, current outstanding debts, and collateral. You should also know exactly why the loan is needed. If it is a frivolous reason, or if the person hesitates to tell you, do not co-sign—and do *not* be embarrassed to make such inquiries. Anyone who wants you to co-sign a note is asking a big favor and should be willing to provide answers.

If you decide to co-sign, find out the terms of repayment and the total amount to be borrowed. Experts suggest two other steps to take to protect yourself:

1. If the amount you are co-signing for is substantial, or if repaying it will burden you, require that the borrower get credit life and disability insurance. This will protect you in case the borrower dies or is disabled and cannot repay the loan.
2. Talk with the lending institution and ask to be notified if the borrower is ever late with payments, or if he is having trouble meeting the payments. That way at least you can try to head off a default on the loan, or prepare to pay it off yourself.

Credit Card Abuse—Another Word of Caution

Credit card abuse is a major problem all across the country. Millions of cards are lost or stolen each year, and millions of dollars of unauthorized purchases are made on these cards. Under Texas criminal laws, credit card abuse is a third-degree felony, punishable by two to 10 years in the penitentiary and a possible fine of up to $5,000.

Unlawful credit card abuses include: stealing, buying, or selling credit cards; forging signatures on cards; knowingly using an expired card; using a card without the consent of the holder; receiving a stolen credit card; inducing a credit card holder to buy items which he cannot pay for; and many others.

Some estimates indicate that approximately 60 percent of all credit card abuses involve cards that were lost by card-holders or stolen from them. Statistics indicate that cards are lost or stolen most often in hotels, motels, bars and restaurants. They are also stolen by pickpockets, stolen from automobiles, and lost or stolen in the mail.

Consumers are protected in such situations by a federal law which stipulates that a cardholder's maximum liability is $50 for *unauthorized* charges. The credit card issuer must inform you of this liability and must supply you with a self-addressed, stamped notice to use if a card is lost or stolen. The issuer must also be able to prove that unauthorized charges up to $50 were made *before* you notified the company of the loss. If the issuer fails to observe these requirements, you are protected from all liability. The law also requires that cards have your signature, photo, or some other means of identification on them.

One of the best ways to protect yourself from credit card abuse is to cut up and throw away all cards you do not need or use, since you could be required to pay $50 on each lost card if your wallet is lost or stolen.

Also, when you receive a new card, sign it right away. Never lend a credit card to anyone not authorized to use it. At home, keep a list of all your cards, with account numbers and names and addresses of issuers. Compare this list with your cards regularly, and always telephone the issuer immediately if any card is missing. Follow up that notification with a *registered* letter or a telegram. And be sure your card is returned to you after every credit transaction.

You should be alert, too, to signs of possible credit card theft or abuse: A customary monthly bill fails to arrive, indicating someone may have stolen your card and sent in an address change; a renewal card does not arrive before the expiration date on your current card; or perhaps a monthly bill is larger than the total of individual charge slips would indicate, or includes a purchase for which there is no individual charge slip, or a purchase in a different city or town.

Finally, if you suspect credit card abuse, contact your district or county attorney.

Special Legal Rights and Remedies

Because of the rapid growth in the consumer credit market since World War II, both federal and state governments have enacted remedial legislation and regulations to alleviate the abuses that grew with the system. In 1967 the Texas Legislature passed a law which attempts to clearly define interest and usury, regulate credit sales and services, and place limits on the charges imposed in connection with such sales and services. This law requires that specific disclosures be made in consumer credit transactions, and it provides a number of legal remedies for consumers. The federal government also passed a law which, including amendments and regulations, now covers the following consumer credit concerns: truth in lending, billing disputes, equal credit opportunity, fair credit reporting, and consumer leases. Taken together, the state and federal laws provide many important rights you should be aware of.

Disclosure Requirements

One of the purposes of recent legislation is to inform you of all charges involved in a credit transaction so that you understand the true cost of a purchase. Federal law requires disclosure of the annual percentage rate (APR) in all credit sales to permit comparison of credit terms. Studies have shown that these disclosures have stimulated comparison shopping.

In addition to requiring the use of standardized credit terms, the law requires that creditors make certain specific disclosures prior to or at the time of the sale. Important contract terms must be revealed clearly and conspicuously to avoid surprise by "hidden" clauses. It prohibits deceptive advertising of credit terms. Also, mailing unsolicited credit cards is outlawed.

The disclosure requirements distinguish between closed-end and open-end credit transactions. For closed-end (installment) sales, the creditor must provide descriptions of late-payment charges, delinquent and default charges, the method by which rebates of finance charges will be calculated if the loan is repaid early, any penalties for early repayment, and the secured property, if any. The following major costs must also be itemized and disclosed: the purchase price of the goods or services, the amount of the finance charge, the amount of the down payment or trade-in allowance, the amount financed, the size and due dates of monthly payments, and any additional charges.

A simpler disclosure method is required for open-end transactions (credit cards, charge accounts). The following information must appear on each credit card or charge account billing: the monthly interest rate, the method used for calculating the account balance upon which the finance charge is levied, the conditions upon which finance charges will be made, the method for figuring the finance charge, a monthly statement of the accounts, and the date by which payment is required to avoid additional finance charges.

Both criminal and civil penalties may be enforced against creditors who violate the federal law. Also, both federal and state law provide the right to file a private lawsuit, and it looks as if consumers are taking advantage of this right. Over 2,000 federal consumer credit lawsuits were filed in 1976 alone! If you win such a suit, there is a mandatory civil penalty of twice the amount of the finance charge involved, with a minimum allowable recovery of $100 and a maximum of $1,000. Also, if you win you are awarded court costs and reasonable attorney's fees. In a criminal lawsuit, creditors who willingly and knowingly violate the law may be fined up to $5,000 or sent to prison for up to one year, or both.

Billing Disputes

In October 1975, a new federal law went into effect which is designed to resolve billing disputes fairly by helping to alleviate the problems caused by the many clerical and mechanical errors made on periodic billing statements. The law applies only to open-end credit plans such as credit cards and charge accounts—*not* to installment loans or purchases.

Basically, creditors are required to acknowledge your inquiry about a billing statement and promptly correct errors or explain why the statement is correct. Open-end creditors must explain the dispute settlement procedure to you. Figure 5-1 is an example of the information that must, according to the Federal Trade Commission, be given to open-end credit customers.

To start the billing dispute procedure, you must send a written notice describing the error within 60 days of receipt of the billing statement. All of the following are considered billing errors:

1. Accounting errors;
2. Failure to credit the account for payments made or goods returned;
3. Billings that need further explanation;
4. Charges not made, or charges made by an unauthorized person;
5. Charges for goods not delivered as agreed or which were not accepted;
6. Charges billed with an incorrect description, date or amount;
7. Failures to bill the consumer at the correct address, provided that the creditor was given a change of address notice at least 10 days prior to the billing.

Your billing inquiry must be acknowledged within 30 days and settled within 90 days. Prior to settlement, creditors cannot send you harassing letters and may not close your account during that time for refusal to pay the disputed amount. They are forbidden to issue bad credit reports unless you are notified and credit bureaus are informed that the bill is in dispute. In such cases, you must be sent the names of all who receive notice of the delinquent debt. If the company later discovers it was in error, it must report the bill's settlement to everyone who received notice of the delinquency.

Problems with defective merchandise or bad service are not "billing errors." However, you should be aware of certain rights in connection with credit card purchases. In the past, you were not permitted to withhold payment to credit card issuers when goods were defective. Now, the law allows you to withhold payment until the matter is settled,

The Federal Truth in Lending Act requires prompt correction of billing mistakes.

1. If you want to preserve your rights under the Act, here's what to do if you think your bill is wrong or if you need more information about an item on your bill:

a. Do not write on the bill. On a separate sheet of paper write (you may telephone your inquiry but doing so will not preserve your rights under this law) the following:

i. Your name and account number (if any).

ii. A description of the error and an explanation (to the extent you can explain) why you believe it is an error. If you only need more information, explain the item you are not sure about and, if you wish, ask for evidence of the charge such as a copy of the charge slip. Do not send in your copy of a sales slip or other document unless you have a duplicate copy for your records.

iii. The dollar amount of the suspected error.

iv. Any other information (such as your address) which you think will help American Express Company to identify you or the reason for your complaint or inquiry.

b. Send your billing error notice to the address on your bill which is listed after the words: "Send Inquiries To:" Mail it as soon as you can, but in any case, early enough to reach American Express Company within 60 days (residents of California see note) after the bill was mailed to you.

2. American Express must acknowledge all letters pointing out possible errors within 30 days of receipt, unless American Express is able to correct your bill during that 30 days. Within 90 days after receiving your letter, American Express must either correct the error or explain why American Express believes the bill was correct. Once American Express has explained the bill, American Express has no further obligation to you even though you still believe that there is an error, except as provided in paragraph 5 below.

3. After American Express has been notified, neither American Express nor an attorney nor a collection agency may send you collection letters or take other collection action with respect to the amount in dispute; but periodic statements may be sent to you, and the disputed amount can be applied against your credit limit. You cannot be threatened with damage to your credit rating or sued for the amount in question, nor can the disputed amount be reported to a credit bureau or to other creditors as delinquent until American Express has answered your inquiry. However, you remain obligated to pay the parts of your bill not in dispute.

4. If it is determined that American Express has made a mistake on your bill, you will not have to pay any finance charge on any disputed amount. If it turns out that American Express has not made an error, you may have to pay finance charges on the amount in dispute, and you will have to make up any missed minimum or required payments on the disputed amount. Unless you have agreed that your bill was correct, American Express must send you a written notification of what you owe; and if it is determined that American Express did make a mistake in billing the disputed amount, you must be given the time to pay which you normally are given to pay undisputed amounts before any more finance charges or late payment charges on the disputed amount can be charged to you.

5. If the American Express explanation does not satisfy you and you notify American Express in writing within 10 days after you receive their explanation that you still refuse to pay the disputed amount, American Express may report you to credit bureaus and other creditors and may pursue regular collection procedures. But American Express must also report that you think you do not owe the money, and American Express must let you know to whom such reports were made. Once the matter has been settled between you and American Express, American Express must notify those to whom they reported you as delinquent of the subsequent resolution.

6. If American Express does not follow these rules, American Express is not allowed to collect the first $50 of the disputed amount and finance charges, even if the bill turns out to be correct.

7. If you have a problem with property or services purchased with a credit card, you may have the right not to pay the remaining amount due on them, if you first try in good faith to return them or give the merchant a chance to correct the problem. There are two limitations on this right:

a. You must have bought them in your home state or if not within your home state within 100 miles of your current mailing address; and

b. The purchase must have been more than $50.

However, these limitations do not apply if the merchant is owned or operated by American Express, or if American Express mailed you the advertisement for the property or services.

NOTE: Residents of California—The laws of your State allow you a longer period of time. Reliance upon the longer time period available under state law may result in your losing important rights which could be preserved by acting more promptly under federal law. Such state law provisions shall only become operative upon the expiration of the time period permitted under federal law for submitting a proper written notification of a billing error.

Figure 5-1. The Federal Trade Commission requires that a Billing Information Notice such as this be given to open-end credit customers to explain dispute settlement procedures. (Courtesy of American Express Company.)

provided the item cost more than $50 and was bought in your home state or within 100 miles of your home.

During a billing dispute, you may withhold only the amount of money in dispute. Once settled, you can be required to pay finance charges accumulated on the disputed balance if the bill was correct; if the bill was incorrect, you must be given the usual amount of time to pay the corrected amount without finance charges or late fees.

If the creditor does not follow the prescribed dispute settlement procedure, the first $50 of the disputed amount cannot be collected, even if the bill was correct. Also, you may sue the creditor for violating the law and may win minimum damages of $100, court costs, and reasonable attorney's fees.

Equal Credit Opportunity

Both federal and Texas laws provide certain guarantees concerning the availability of credit to consumers. Effective in October 1975, federal law prohibits discrimination in any aspect of a credit transaction based on sex or marital status, and since March 1977 it prohibits discrimination based on race, national origin, religion, age (with some limited exceptions), receipt of money from a public assistance program (Social Security, Aid to Dependent Children, food stamps, etc.), or good faith exercise of rights under the other federal laws. The law applies to all creditors who regularly extend credit, including banks, small loan and finance companies, retail and department stores, credit card companies and credit unions. However, it guarantees creditors the right to deny credit to consumers who are not found "credit-worthy" for financial reasons.

Since Texas is a *community property* state, creditors may request an applicant's spouse to sign any legal documents that may later be needed in levying on property for unpaid accounts. However, applicants must be given the option of whether to designate a title (Mr., Ms., Mrs., Miss), and they have the right to have accounts listed in either the married name, maiden name or both. Creditors are prohibited from asking about your plans to have or raise children, but may ask about the number of dependents in your family and some questions about child support payments. Another practice by creditors, the "discounting" of a woman's income by a certain percentage before judging crediworthiness, also has been outlawed.

In the past, widows and divorcees had a difficult time obtaining credit because family credit accounts were typically listed in the husband's name. Thus, the widow or divorcee was denied credit for lack of a "credit history." Creditors are now required to report information on accounts shared in the names of both spouses. Also, spouses have the right to prove that a shared account does not accurately reflect their ability or willingness to repay debts. Because of these new legal rights and the increasing importance of credit in today's economy, women who are divorced, married, separated or widowed should make sure that all of the relevant credit information at local credit bureaus is in a file under their names.

Questions concerning age may not be asked unless the answers will be used to favor the applicant or to determine other relevant factors, such as whether impending retirement will significantly reduce the ability to repay a debt. Creditors cannot refuse to extend credit because of your race or national origin or, in the case of a home repair loan, the predominant race in your neighborhood. It *is* legal to ask about permanent residence and immigration status and to consider that information in granting or denying credit.

Creditors are forbidden to automatically cancel a credit account due to a name or marital status change, the reaching of a certain age, or retirement. The government requires home mortgage lenders to ask questions about marital status, race and national origin to assist it in monitoring compliance with the laws. But you are not *required* to answer such questions, and credit cannot be denied on the basis of their answers.

You are now entitled to be informed of the results of your application for credit within 30 days of its receipt by the creditor. Refusals must either list specific reasons for the credit denial or inform you that specific reasons will be given, upon request, within 60 days. Most credit application results must be given in writing, but very small credit businesses may give oral notices of refusal.

If you believe you have been discriminated against, you have the right to sue in federal court and receive actual damages, court costs, reasonable attorney's fees and punitive damages up to $10,000. Texas law also prohibits sex discrimination in credit transactions, and you are permitted to recover either actual damages caused by the denial or $50, whichever is greater, and court costs.

Credit Reporting

Federal law protects consumers against the circulation of inaccurate or obsolete credit information and ensures that credit reporting agencies exercise their responsibilities fairly and equitably. Anyone with a charge account, home mortgage, or life insurance policy or who has applied for a personal loan or a job has a credit record. If you have a credit file, it is likely to contain all of the following: identifying information; current employment; personal history such as birthdate, dependents, etc.; credit history, including the promptness with which bills are paid; information publicly available, including arrests, indictments, convictions, tax liens, divorce, death, marriage, bankruptcies and court judgments.

The law guarantees you the right to be given the name and address of the credit bureau which prepared a report that results in the denial of credit or an increase in the cost of credit or insurance. You have the right to be informed of the "nature and substance" of the credit information in your file, although you need not physically be given the file. This information must be given for free if you were denied credit, but a small fee can be charged if you are just looking. You also have the right to take someone along when examining the credit record. Also, the credit bureau must tell you the names and addresses of anyone who received a credit report for the past six months, or for two years in the case of employers who received credit information.

When there is a dispute about information in a file, the bureau can be required to reinvestigate and delete the information if it is inaccurate or cannot be verified. In such cases you can demand that the reporting agency notify anyone who received incorrect information of the change, at no charge to you. Further, you have the right to have your version of the dispute placed in the file and included in future credit reports. The law also protects you against the reporting of obsolete information by requiring that adverse information older than seven years not be reported; bankruptcies, however, may be reported for 14 years.

Investigative reports differ from credit reports in that they contain more personal information, gathered from friends and neighbors, concerning your character, general reputation and lifestyle. This type of report is used most often by potential employers and insurance companies. You have the right to know the "nature and substance" of this type of file but not to know who provided the information. As with the credit report you have the right to request the names and addresses of everyone who has received an investigative report on you for the past six months, or two years in the case of an employer.

Credit reporting agencies who violate the law can be sued for actual damages, any extra penalty the court awards, court costs and reasonable attorney's fees. Also, criminal penalties of a maximum fine of $5,000 or one year in prison, or both, may be assessed.

Texas Consumer Credit Regulatory Agencies

A number of federal and state agencies oversee the lending institutions of Texas. The main Texas agencies are the Finance Commission, which controls the Department of Banking, the Savings and Loan Department, and the Office of the Consumer Credit Commissioner, and the Credit Union Department.

Finance Commission of Texas

The Commission is made up of a nine-member board, appointed by the Governor with the approval of the Senate. There is a banking section, made up of six members; four who are active bankers and two with recognized business ability. The Savings and Loan Department has three members, two who are building and loan executives and one who has recognized business ability.

The Commission is charged with providing overall supervisory control of the following agencies: the Department of Banking, the Savings and Loan Department, and the Office of the Consumer Credit Commissioner. In addition, the Commission makes special study recommendations for more effective savings-and-loan and banking laws in the state.

Department of Banking
2601 North Lamar
Austin, TX 78705
(512) 475-4451

The banking department is supervised by the State Banking Board, which is composed of three members—two ex officio members and a third appointed by the Governor with the approval of the Senate. The Banking Commissioner serves as chairperson of the Board and is the administrative head of the banking department. The commissioner acts as the receiver of insolvent banks. The department's duties are to administer the laws regulating trust companies and state banks; certain funeral and cemetary contracts; and the sale of money orders, checks or drafts. It reviews bank examiners' reports and takes corrective actions against banks and bank officials.

Savings and Loan Department
1004 Lavaca
Austin, TX 78701
(512) 475-7991

The Savings and Loan Department is run by the Savings and Loan Commissioner, who is selected by the Finance Commission with the approval of the Senate. It regulates state-chartered savings-and-loan associations, reviews applications for new associations and branches, and removes directors or officers who violate regulations.

Credit Union Department
1106 Clayton Lane
Suite 206-East
Twin Towers Bldg.
Austin, TX 78723
(512) 475-2296

The Credit Union Department is run by a six-member board appointed by the Governor with the approval of the Senate. The members are all required to have at least five years of credit union management experience with state-chartered credit unions. The Credit Union Commissioner is the administrative head of the department. Its duties involve issuing charters, supervising state credit unions, and monitoring compliance with state regulations.

Office of the Consumer Credit Commissioner
P.O. Box 2107
Austin, TX 78768
(512) 475-2111

This agency is supervised by the Consumer Credit Commissioner, who is appointed by the Finance Commission of Texas. It is charged with administering the Texas Credit Code. It licenses and regulates the personal finance and small loan companies that handle a great portion of the consumer credit transactions in the state: pawnshops, consumer finance companies, and insurance premium finance companies. The office handles complaints regarding retail credit sales and motor vehicle credit sales and is charged with promoting consumer credit education in the state.

Federal Consumer Credit Regulatory Agencies

In addition to supervision by the Department of Banking of Texas, state-chartered banks that belong to the Federal Reserve System must conform to standards set by the Board of Governors of the Federal Reserve System. Also, state-chartered banks insured by the Federal Deposit Insurance Corporation (FDIC) are subject to its regulation. There are two other federal agencies particularly concerned with regulating consumer credit lending institutions in Texas: the Comptroller of the Currency and the Federal Trade Commission.

Comptroller of the Currency
Consumer Affairs Division
Washington, D.C. 20219
(202) 566-2000

The Comptroller oversees the nationally chartered banks in the state. The office's approval is needed for the organization of new banks and reorganization of existing banks. Also, it examines national banks periodically with its nationwide staff of over 2,000 bank examiners.

Federal Trade Commission
Sixth and Pennsylvania Ave. S.W.
Washington, D.C. 20580
(202) 962-5664

Dallas Regional Office
2001 Bryan Street
Dallas, TX 75201
(214) 749-3057

The Federal Trade Commission (FTC) is the federal agency most concerned with consumer credit. It is charged with keeping competition free and fair in the United States by preventing monopolies, restraints or trade, or deceptive or unfair trade practices. The FTC monitors compliance with the federal Consumer Protection Act, including its components: the Truth in Lending Act, the Fair Credit Reporting Act, the Fair Credit Billing Act, the Equal Credit Opportunity Act, and the Consumer Leasing Act.

Debt Collection

People who do not pay their debts fall into three categories: (1) those who will not pay, regardless of their situation; (2) those who are unable to pay; and (3) those who refuse to pay because of some complaint related to the debt.

Everyone agrees that if a person is able to pay a just debt, he should. But what if you are unable to pay your debts because all available resources are consumed by more important debts such as food, clothing, shelter or medical care? What if you refuse to pay a debt because the product you purchased is defective or because the purchase was solicited by fraud? Regardless of the category into which a debtor falls, the business is left in the same position: a product or service has been delivered but not paid for. No business can survive if its customers do not pay.

Our laws attempt to reconcile or satisfy these different needs. To the protesting consumer, the law provides a forum for redress by allowing him to sue the business for a defective product or an unlawful practice. To protect the debtor who is unable to pay, the law prevents a creditor from attaching or garnishing wages and salaries to ensure that money needed for necessities cannot be taken. The law also protects a debtor's homestead—his house—and other essentials of life so that a creditor cannot satisfy his claim by thrusting the debtor into the streets.

On the other hand, businesses are given the means to collect just debts through the courts. Often the procedure is relatively simple and efficient, such as the way an automobile purchased on credit is repossessed. At other times the process may not be so simple; nevertheless, the procedure is there for a business to resort to for help.

Texas law also assures all citizens that unfair or unjust debt collection practices will not be used against them. If such practices are attempted, the law provides an effective means of stopping them quickly.

Who Collects Debts?

When a debt is "turned over for collection," it is generally either given to a professional debt collection agency or to an individual debt collector. In other words, the business with whom the consumer dealt to create the debt leaves the picture and the debt collector takes over. The reason for this is that the time required to collect debts would leave most businesses little time for anything else.

Debt collection is big business indeed. In 1977 over $5 *billion* in outstanding debts was turned over to collection agencies.

Most consumers who obtain credit fully intend to repay their debts. When a default occurs, it is nearly always due to unforeseen circumstances such as unemployment, overextension, serious illness or marital difficulties. Nevertheless, because of the tremendous amount of money turned over for collection each year, Congress has found default on consumer debt to be a national problem.

Informal Debt Collection Practices

When you owe a debt that is past due, the debt collector will begin his attempts at collection through *informal* means; that is, you will not be taken to court immediately. Instead, you will receive a series of "dunning" letters or telephone calls encouraging you to pay the debt. Informal means are used because they are much less expensive than a lawsuit.

Dunning Letters

A dunning letter is any written communication demanding payment of a debt. Most collection agencies use a series of dunning letters, starting with gentle reminders and ending with a threatening demand. The sample letters that follow illustrate the normal sequence:

(Text continued on page 113)

ABC COLLECTION AGENCY

August 1, 1979

Dear

  We are a large collection agency. Your book club
has engaged us to collect your debt of $27.10.

  Due to the circumstances of your account, we have
not notified an attorney about it.

  Instead, we are attempting to get you to voluntarily
pay this debt.

  We assume that you will pay immediately. If
we do not receive your check or money order by August 17 ,
we will proceed with collection procedures.

Yours truly,

Collection Agent

ABC COLLECTION AGENCY

August 20, 1979

Dear

It is difficult to understand why you have not paid your $27.10 debt owed to your book club.

If you think that this debt is unjust, you may want to retain an attorney to advise you on this question.

If you do not dispute this debt, you have a legal and moral obligation to pay it now.

As stated in our first letter, we are a large collection agency and your book club has engaged us to collect your debt. We will go ahead with our collection procedures unless you send us your check or money order for $27.10 by September 4 .

Yours truly,

Collection Agent

ABC COLLECTION AGENCY

September 7, 1979

Dear

    We have written you twice about the $27.10 debt you owe your book club, and you have failed to respond.

    We must know what you plan to do.

    We must hear from you or your attorney, even if you don't think you can repay this debt now or you don't believe you owe this bill.

    If you do not answer us, we will have no choice but to initiate collection procedures.

    We will expect your check or reply by return mail.

Yours truly,

Collection Agent

ABC COLLECTION AGENCY

                                    September 14, 1979

Dear

        What do you want us to do next?

        The choice is yours...

        We must have $27.10 to pay your account in full.

                            Yours truly,

                            Collection Agent

ABC COLLECTION AGENCY

October 1, 1979

Dear

Our computer tells us that you still owe $27.10 to your book club. Since you have ignored us so far, we assume that you do owe this debt, and we intend to collect it from you.

Your debts and this collection agency will not go away just because you ignore us. Since you have refused to pay, we must protect our client.

Therefore, this is your final notice from us before we forward your account to our attorney.

If we receive your payment of $27.10 now, we will discontinue collection procedures.

Yours truly,

Collection Agent

The number of dunning letters a debt collector sends before turning an account over to an attorney varies with each agency. Therefore, there is no assurance that you will receive an entire series of letters like these examples before legal action is taken against you.

The examples appear to be lawful dunning letters. That is, there is nothing on the face of the letters that violates the law. But even these letters could be unlawful if any of these conditions are not met:

1. The debt must still be owed and not be in dispute.
2. The letters must be truthful.
3. The letters must be part of a genuine attempt to collect a debt and not mailed for the purpose of harassment.

For example, in the last letter, the collection agent threatens to turn the account over to an attorney. If, in fact, the agent has no intentions of turning the account over to an attorney, a letter making that threat is unlawful.

Some dunning letters are obviously unlawful. For instance, letters that simulate or are designed to look like legal instruments—papers issued by a court or governmental agency—are illegal. Dunning letters which falsely state that a court has judged the debt to be valid are likewise unlawful. In fact, any dunning letter that misrepresents either the law or the facts of a transaction violates both state and federal law. Figures 6-1, 6-2 and 6-3 illustrate types of dunning letters which are unlawful.

If you receive a dunning letter you believe to be unlawful, contact the business to whom you owe the debt. Most businesses do not tolerate unlawful practices by people who collect debts for them. After all, the debt collectors' practices tend to reflect on the business. And, if a business knows its debt collector is using unlawful means to collect debts, it may be held equally responsible for those practices. Of course, you will also want to contact the Texas Attorney General's Consumer Protection Division to make sure that the same unlawful practices are not used on others.

Telephone Calls

Experience has shown that the chances of receiving prompt payment are much better if a debt collector can make personal contact with the

---

DEBTOR ON NOTICE

IN THE CLAIM OF)

_____
CREDITOR
VS.

_____
DEBTOR

You are hereby advised of a VALID CLAIM against you for the amount of $_____
for account due_____
This claim is now overdue, and if payment is not made or satisfactory arrangements made
with creditor on or before the_____day of _____19____it shall be
just cause for the creditor to protect his rights in accordance with all laws, together with
interest and cost.

AFFIDAVIT OF CLAIM

The above creditor hereby certifies that audit has been made in the above mentioned
claim and has found the account to be true and correct as shown by his records to the best
of his knowledge and belief.

_____
Creditor or Agent

Subscribed and affirmed before me this_____day of

_____, 19 ____.

_____
Notary Public or Witness

ALL RIGHTS RESERVED

Figure 6-1. An unlawful dunning letter. It is illegal for a dunning letter to
appear as if it is a paper issued by a court or government agency.

debtor over the telephone. Dunning letters may be easily discarded (or
never opened) and forgotten. A telephone call is much more difficult to
ignore.

All legitimate debt collectors keep careful records of telephone calls
made to debtors. At any given moment a legitimate debt collector can
tell you not only how many times you have been called and when, but
the substance of the conversation as well. Therefore, the debt collector's
file on a debtor will be complete regardless of whether letters or the
telephone are used.

DETACH   And Enclose With Payment   TODAY

_____
(Final Date)

1

Creditor_____ _____

_____ ____ _____

Amount $ 10.06 _____

CHECKS POST DATED FIFTEEN (15) DAYS IN ADVANCE ACCEPTABLE

PREPARATORY LISTING
FOR CIVIL COURT

Before the creditor files suit against you, which would show your name on the court records as a defendant in an action involving non-payment of a debt and having citation issued, we are taking this final step to strongly recommend that you mail your check to this office immediately. Should funds not be readily available, may we suggest that you contact a reputable lending institution to secure the entire amount to pay this indebtedness.

Should we not hear from you within 72 hours, it will be presumed that you do not wish to settle this claim without court action and we will be forced to recommend to our client that proceedings be started at once.

Figure 6-2. _Any dunning letter which threatens court action must be legitimate. If consumers are rarely or never sued by the debt collecter then the use of this form is unlawful._

Pre-emptory Draft   **Value Received**

Demand is hereby made upon you for payment, on or before
of the total sum, past due, shown on statement made a part of this Pre-emptory Draft.

You are hereby notified that, in the event this Pre-emptory Draft is not honored within the time allowed, legal action will be recommended to enforce payment, without further notice to you. The courts prefer that just debts be resolved in an amicable manner, without
judicial decree, when ever possible.

DEBTOR   CREDITOR

Creditor's Statement

$ 10.06

NOTICE

Unless this draft is promptly honored, all expenses for legal action
may be added to the above a-
mount.

—IMPORTANT — GIVE IMMEDIATE ATTENTION —

This private notice is prior to further action

COLLECTION SERVICE COMPANY

Gentlemen:
No further action is necessary. The amount of _____, in full settlement of the above claim, is herewith enclosed.
See that I am given proper credit.

NAME_____

ADDRESS_____

☛ To insure proper credit to your account, send balance in the enclosed envelope.

Figure **6-3.** *In consumer transactions there is no such thing as a "Pre-emptory Draft." This document is therefore, nothing more than a dunning letter. A consumer may agree to pay a debt, but there is no agreement to honor this "draft."*

As with dunning letters, there are legal and illegal ways in which the telephone can be used to collect debts. There is nothing wrong with a debt collector calling you at a reasonable time and place to demand payment of a debt, but the debt collector violates the law if he does any of the following:

1. Uses any false, misleading or deceptive representations.
2. Calls at an unusual time or place (all calls should be between 8 a.m. and 9 p.m.).
3. Calls your place of employment if he knows, or should know, that the employer prohibits the debtor from receiving such communications.

Telephone Log Of Debt Collector Calls			
Date	**Time**	**Identity of Caller**	**Substance of Conversation**

Figure 6-4. *Use a telephone log sheet similar to this to keep a written record of the debt collector's calls. To prove telephone harassment, you must have accurate notes on the time, place, and substance of these conversations.*

4. Calls you after he has been advised that you are represented by an attorney.

Telephone harassment by a debt collector is very difficult to prove because the entire experience is verbal—you get nothing in writing from the debt collector. Unlike dunning letters, which can be physically examined, what was said in a telephone call likely will end up being your word against the debt collector's, and the debt collector will have meticulous self-made notes to back up his claims.

Because of the difficulty of proving telephone harassment, you should do two things. First, if a debt collector makes harassing telephone calls, make yourself a log (Figure 6-4) so you can keep accurate notes of the time, place, and substance of the conversations. Also, try to find out the name of the caller. If a debt collector refuses to identify himself or the agency for whom he is calling, he violates the law.

Unlawful Practices

When informal debt collection procedures are begun against you, look over the following list of illegal practices to make sure you are not being victimized.

First, a debt collector cannot use *threats or coercion* to collect a debt. In other words, he cannot:

1. Use or threaten to use violence or other criminal means to collect a debt.
2. Falsely accuse you of fraud or other crimes.
3. Tell other people that you are refusing to pay an undisputed debt if the debt is in dispute *and* you have notified the creditor of the dispute.
4. Threaten to sell or assign your debt to a third party and then tell you that by selling your debt to this third party you will lose all defenses you may have to paying the debt.
5. Threaten that you will be arrested for not paying the debt.
6. Threaten to file criminal charges against you when you have not violated any criminal law. Non-payment of a debt violates no criminal law!
7. Threaten to seize, repossess or sell any of your property without proper court proceedings, unless your contract with the creditor gives him this right.

A debt collector also is prohibited from *harassing, abusing or unduly annoying* someone who owes a debt. That is, the debt collector cannot:

1. Use profane or obscene language in talking with you.
2. Call you on the telephone without telling you his name.
3. Cause expense to you by means of collect long distance telephone charges, telegram fees and the like without first disclosing the name of the person making the call.
4. Make continuous and repeated telephone calls with the intent of harassing you.

A debt collector cannot use *unfair or "unconscionable"* means to collect a debt. Admittedly, unfair and unconscionable are very general terms. Therefore, to make sure everyone knows what they mean, the law limits their meaning to these two situations:

1. A debt collector cannot ask for a written statement which falsely states that the debt was incurred for necessaries of life such as clothing, food or medicine. (If you sign such a statement, the debt collector may be able to seize property which would otherwise be exempt.)
2. A debt collector cannot collect or attempt to collect any extra charges, interest, or expenses on a debt unless you have agreed with the creditor that these expenses may be collected.

Finally, a debt collector cannot make *fraudulent, deceptive or misleading representations* to a person who owes a debt. Specifically, he cannot:

1. Use a name other than the true name of the business or true personal name of the collector.
2. Fail to disclose to you that he is attempting to collect a debt.
3. Misrepresent the character or amount of your debt, or misrepresent the status of a debt in any judicial proceeding. In other words, a debt collector cannot falsely tell you that a court has ordered you to pay a debt.
4. Falsely state that he or his agency is bonded or affiliated with any local, state or federal official or agency.
5. Use any written communication that gives the impression that it is a document issued by a court or government agency.
6. Tell you that your debt may be increased by attorney's fees or collection fees, interest or other charges, unless a contract or statute permits the fees.
7. Tell you that your debt will definitely be increased by attorney's fees or other fees when such fees are discretionary with a court.
8. Falsely represent that an attorney is collecting your debt.
9. Use any written communication that violates the United States Postal laws or regulations.
10. Falsely represent that your debt is being collected by an independent debt collection agency when the debt actually is being collected by an organization or person under the control of the creditor.

Skip Tracing

Some consumers run out on their debts. After borrowing money or purchasing goods or services on credit, these individuals pack up their belongings and move on to parts unknown. Many credit bureaus and debt collectors offer a debtor-locating service, called "skip tracing," to help businesses victimized in this way.

Skip tracing is done in a variety of ways. Since many credit bureaus and debt collection agencies are nationwide companies, they will alert other offices to watch for the debtor's name to see if it appears in their files. Court and driver's license records may be checked. One of the most commonly used skip tracing techniques is to send mail to the debtor's former address, return receipt requested, in hope that the debtor will accept delivery at his forwarding address. This mail often is disguised so the debtor will not know a collection agency or credit bureau is looking for him.

Skip tracing obviously is a valuable service. A business stands no chance of collecting a just debt if it cannot locate the debtor. But debt collectors and credit bureaus who engage in skip tracing activities must follow certain rules to minimize the risks of embarrassment:

1. When a debtor is identified by name, only confirming and correcting location information can be given. The debtor's employer cannot be identified unless the creditor specifically requests this.
2. No mention of the debt can be made.
3. The debt collector or credit bureau cannot communicate with anyone more than once.
4. The debt collector or credit bureau cannot use symbols or language that identifies itself as being in the debt collection business.
5. No post cards may be used.
6. If the alleged debtor has an attorney, the debt collector or credit bureau must deal with that attorney and not the consumer.

Formal Debt Collection Procedures

When informal debt collection procedures do not work, the creditor can resort to several *formal* procedures, so labeled because the ways of using them are spelled out quite clearly by the law—two of them require using the courts. The three principal procedures creditors use when informal methods do not work are *repossession, foreclosure* and *litigation.*

Repossession

We most often think of repossession in connection with automobiles. But whenever you purchase goods in which the seller retains a *security interest* (see page 85), the seller normally has the right to repossess those goods if they are not paid for as agreed. A security interest (also called a "purchase money security interest") in consumer goods may be taken by a person who either (1) sells the goods to a consumer on credit or (2) advances money to enable a consumer to purchase goods.

Most contracts that give the seller or the bank a security interest provide that the goods can be repossessed without going to court—the seller or his agent can go to the location of the goods and pick them up. Most people who repossess automobiles try to do so at a time and place that avoid direct confrontation with the consumer. After all, people do not like a total stranger driving "their" car away. Hence, we hear of such things happening when the lights are out and everyone is asleep. The truth is, most repossessions occur in broad daylight in people's driveways, but the dark-of-the-night stories sound better.

A person who repossesses consumer goods cannot "breach the peace" in doing so. This means that no harm can be done to persons or property. If a breach of the peace is necessary to get the goods, the creditor must go to court and obtain a court order for the sheriff to pick up the goods.

When goods are repossessed, the law requires the creditor to give the consumer an opportunity to pay off the debt and reclaim the goods. When you have paid 60 percent or more of the cash price of the goods, the creditor does not have the option of simply keeping the goods and cancelling your debt. Instead, he must sell the goods within 90 days of repossession. If the goods are not sold within 90 days, you may sue the creditor.

After the repossessed goods are sold, the amount of money made from the sale must be applied to satisfy your debt. Any balance left over must be paid to you. If there is not enough money made from the sale to pay the debt off, then the creditor may sue *you* to recover the balance.

Foreclosure

In most real estate sales the person or company financing the sale (mortgagor) has the right to foreclose on the property of the borrower (mortgagee) if the mortgage payments are not made.

The mortgagor's right to foreclose generally is spelled out in a *deed of trust* which you sign when you buy a house. Most deeds of trust provide that in the event of default, the mortgagor has the right to sell your property (without going to court) to satisfy the unpaid balance of your mortgage. If there is any excess left over from the sale, it must be paid to you.

Usually, however, there is not enough money realized from the sale to cover the balance of your mortgage payments. When this occurs, the mortgagor has the right to sue you to obtain a *deficiency judgment.* The amount of this judgment is the difference between the amount realized from the foreclosure sale and the debt owed.

Litigation

Whenever you do not pay your debts, as agreed, the creditor can file a lawsuit to recover the balance due. But because this option is costly, creditors use it less frequently than the debt collection practices previously discussed.

The variety of lawsuits over debts owed is tremendous, so a detailed discussion of all such suits is impossible. Instead, the two best things you can do when you are sued are recommended below:

1. Get a Lawyer. If you are sued in any court other than a small claims court, retain an attorney if at all possible. There is an old saying among lawyers, "Any attorney who represents himself has a fool for a client." The same is doubly true for you if you have no legal training. Our court system operates under highly technical rules. The rules of evidence, the law of the case, the strict rules relating to *what* you can say in court and *when* you can say it—all are complex and often confusing. It takes many years of legal training and experience to even begin mastering the art of trying a lawsuit. Don't sell yourself or your case short by not seeking professional help.

2. Do Not Delay. As soon as you are served with process (the plaintiff's petition), begin taking steps to defend yourself. In most cases you have only 20 days within which to answer the allegations made against you in the lawsuit. If you fail to answer the lawsuit by filing papers in court, the plaintiff may get a *default judgment* against you. A default judgment has the same force and effect as if you had gone to trial and the other side won. Behind such a judgment is the court's assumption that if you are sued and you fail to answer, the plaintiff's allegations must be true. You can avoid a default judgment by contacting your lawyer quickly.

In most litigation, none of your property or money can be affected until the lawsuit is finished and a *judgment* against you has been entered. However, in debt collection matters, there are some exceptions to this rule. Three procedures allow a creditor to deprive you of the possession and use of certain property or money after a lawsuit is filed but *before* a judgment is entered. These procedures are *garnishment, replevin and sequestration,* and *attachment.*

Garnishment. A garnishment action notifies a third party that the creditor claims the right to specific property or funds belonging to you but in the third party's possession. For example, if you have a checking account and you are sued for a delinquent debt, the creditor may garnish the checking account by having the court order the bank to keep the funds until the lawsuit is completed. This procedure protects the creditor by ensuring that funds will be available out of which the judgment can be satisfied.

In Texas your salary or wages cannot be garnished. That is, an employer cannot be ordered to hold your salary or wages pending the outcome of the creditor's lawsuit against you. However, any money in your bank account can be garnished.

Replevin and Sequestration. These actions only affect *specific* property that a creditor claims a right to or an interest in. Again, these procedures may be employed after a lawsuit has been filed but before a final judgment has been entered.

To illustrate these procedures, assume, for example, that you purchase a diamond ring on credit. After making a few payments, you default on the debt and the creditor files a lawsuit against you. Because a diamond ring is easily sold, the creditor may want to ensure that the ring is still in your possession when the lawsuit against you is over. In this situation, he would ask the court to order the sheriff to take possession of the ring and hold it until the lawsuit is completed.

Attachment. Attachment differs from replevin and sequestration in that it can be used by a creditor against all *nonexempt* property of a debtor. That is, once the creditor files a lawsuit against you, he may ask the court to order the sheriff to attach your property or bank accounts so that your assets will be preserved until the end of the lawsuit. Once a judgment is entered, your creditor is assured of having a source of money from which to satisfy his claim.

Generally, you can prevent the use of any of these procedures by filing a bond in a sufficient amount with the court.

These prejudgment procedures serve a purpose in addition to assuring the creditor of a source of money to satisfy a judgment. They put pressure on the debtor to pay the creditor's claim quickly. Few people can live in a normal fashion when their bank accounts are frozen. Consequently, the procedures are quite effective.

Insurance

If you had to select some point in recorded history as the beginning of insurance, it would probably be around the year 1925 B.C., with the compilation of the *Code of Hammurabi*. The *Code* included laws dealing with the no-fault loss of goods-in-transit by a sales agent. Insurance in its modern form was first available in the fourteenth century when, in 1347, the first policy of "modern" marine or transit insurance was written on a vessel in Genoa.

The insurance industry has come a long way since the *Code of Hammurabi*. According to the *Texas Business Review* (July 1978), the Texas insurance industry nearly tripled in size in the last decade alone. From 1966 through 1976, the industry grew from $2.6 billion in premium volume to $7.8 billion. During this same period, benefits paid by insurers and insuring associations more than tripled, increasing from $1.45 billion to $4.73 billion.

We are buying a great deal of insurance. What these and other figures do not reveal, however, is precisely how little most people know about what it is they are buying and whether they have been subjected to unlawful insurance practices. This chapter is intended as a first step toward understanding insurance coverage, terminology, and unlawful insurance practices. It describes the types of insurance coverage most of us buy: life, health, property and personal liability, and automobile, and it gives pointers on shopping for the best coverage, agent and company. Another section explains several insurance practices that are against the law in Texas—while most agents and companies are reputable, you should be able to spot the few who are not.

Finally, this chapter describes the state agency primarily responsible for regulating the insurance industry: the State Board of Insurance.

Types of Insurance

All insurance, regardless of the risks it covers, has certain common features. First, all forms of insurance are contracts in which one party, the *insurer*, promises to pay money or provide a service to another party, the *insured*, when the insured suffers a loss because of a hazard or peril. The underlying function of all insurance is the same: to substitute certainty for uncertainty in the event of some disaster. The effect is to spread the risk, which would normally fall upon one individual, over the members of a large group exposed to the same risk or loss.

While the terms of insurance policies vary tremendously, they all contain the following basic parts:

1. *Declarations* that set forth the persons, property, places and periods of time covered.
2. *Insuring agreement*, a very broad statement that often begins, "In consideration of. . ." and sets forth the formal agreement to provide protection for certain perils in exchange for a certain premium.
3. *Exclusions* that remove certain persons, property and perils from the coverage of the policy.
4. *Conditions*, the ground rules that govern the actions of the parties to the contract, most often dealing with such items as reporting losses, appraisals, cancellations, *subrogation* (allowing the company to sue or take action against someone else to recover the money it paid to you), and applicability of state statutes.

There is now a consumer movement in Texas aimed at simplifying insurance terminology. Almost everyone agrees that insurance policies are extremely confusing. In fact, several learned authors have written volumes to try to explain insurance coverage. This section is not meant to be exhaustive; it is an introduction to insurance terminology and an explanation of the basic types of insurance most of us purchase.

Life Insurance

The thought of our own death is so unpleasant that we tend to spurn the necessary safeguards, such as preparation of a will and settlement of our financial affairs, including the purchase of life insurance (which is actually *death* insurance). As a result, few of us approach the purchase of life insurance as seriously as we approach the purchase of a new car or even a new suit of clothes. We give it little thought, little investigation, and do not proceed with the caution such an important task requires. If consumers are ignorant of the basic facts of life insurance and are reluctant to give serious consideration to real insurance needs, then even the best insurance company and the best agent cannot be as helpful as they should. And it is these consumers who are most likely to fall prey to an unethical company or agent.

The primary purpose of all life insurance is to provide financial protection for the survivors or beneficiaries of the insured after the insured's death. Additionally, many purchasers use life insurance as a means to insure financial security in later years. These purposes cannot be achieved unless consumers purchase the right amount and the right form of insurance protection. But a 1974 Consumers Union Special Report, entitled *A Guide to Life Insurance*, stated that a great many Americans are underinsured and pointed to two causes of this phenomenon: underestimating *how much* life insurance we need and buying policies *inappropriate* to our needs.

Before you shop for life insurance, consider what financial resources will be available to assist your family after your death: for example, income from your spouse, social security, credit union insurance, pension plans, the value of your home, savings and investments, etc. Then compare these resources with the expenses your family will likely incur. Among the costs to take into account are paying off your debts (like doctor and hospital bills, funeral expenses, unpaid taxes), paying off outstanding loans (like the mortgage on your house), college expenses for children, retirement income for your spouse, and day-to-day living costs for your family. Several publications, including the 1972 edition of the *Consumers Union Report on Life Insurance: A Guide to Planning and Buying the Protection You Need*, contain handy worksheets to assist you in approximating how much coverage you will need.

The existence of over 1700 licensed insurers in Texas and the availability of such a vast assortment of policies can make shopping for insurance, and understanding your rights under the policy, a bewildering process. At the most fundamental level, you must understand the two basic forms of life insurance coverage: *whole life* (also called ordinary or straight life) and *term* insurance. Whole life insurance remains in effect as long as you continue to make payments. Term policies, on the other hand, expire after a specified time period unless renewed. Term policies are usually effective for one, five, ten or twenty years.

Term Insurance. The practical distinction between whole life and term policies is that term insurance provides pure death protection only, while whole life combines protection with an investment feature. When you purchase term insurance, you contract with the insurance company for them to pay a specified sum to the person you name as beneficiary should you die during the period the insurance contract is effective.

Term insurance usually is much cheaper than whole life insurance—for the same premium dollar, you can purchase more death protection under term coverage than under whole life coverage. Premiums on term insurance do increase with each renewal, however, and usually jump considerably when you reach age 45. Term insurance is not even available past a certain age, usually 60 to 70.

One of the popular types of term policies is *renewable term*. Under renewable term the face amount of the policy (benefits paid at death) remains fixed, but premiums increase with every renewal. This is because the risk of death increases as you get older. When the policy expires, you do not need a medical examination if you decide to renew your coverage.

Another popular type of term policy is *decreasing term*. Under a decreasing term policy, the premium stays the same each year, but the amount of coverage decreases. Decreasing term insurance may run for a period of 25 years or longer. You get less insurance coverage over time for the same money because your chances of dying increase with each year. The theory behind decreasing term is that, often, maximum benefits are needed during the earlier years of coverage—children are young; or there is a larger mortgage on your home. In fact, decreasing term is frequently sold as *mortgage cancellation insurance,* which insures that the mortgage on your home is paid off in the event of your death. As the mortgage balance decreases with each mortgage payment, the amount of insurance coverage decreases correspondingly.

Term insurance also comes with a *convertibility rider*. This gives you the option, until a specified age, of converting from term insurance to whole life insurance, at a higher premium, without a medical examination.

Whole Life Insurance. This is the oldest and most widely used form of life insurance. It provides protection for as long as you live. You pay a *level premium*: that is, your premiums remain the same, but you must keep paying the premiums for most of your life. With whole life, as opposed to term coverage, you accumulate what is commonly called *cash value, cash surrender value,* or *non-forfeiture value*—money you get back if you give up, or surrender, the policy. The cash value of the policy is low at first but builds up over the years. This cash value of the policy may also be used to secure a low-interest loan, since you can borrow against it.

If, in later years, you feel you no longer need insurance coverage, you have several options under a whole life policy. You can withdraw the savings, or cash value, in either a lump sum or in installments. You can have your policy converted to an *annuity*, which pays a regular monthly income for life. You can also use your cash value for the purchase of extended term coverage in the same amount as the original whole life policy, should premium obligations be difficult to meet. Finally, you can have your policy converted so that it purchases a reduced amount of insurance, paid up for life.

In addition to whole life insurance, companies offer two types of policies that also combine pure insurance with a savings feature: *limited pay life* policies and *endowment policies*. These two types have a stronger investment feature, which means that annual premiums are higher and the cash surrender value increases at a faster rate than under whole life.

Limited Pay Insurance. This is the same as whole life except you pay higher premiums for a limited number of years. Typically, payments are made for 20 or 30 years, until you reach age 60 or 65, when the policy is paid in full and you are protected for the remainder of your life. While, for the same amount of coverage, premiums are higher for limited pay than for whole life, you accumulate a cash value faster under a limited pay policy and can limit the payment of premiums to your earlier years. You can also buy a paid-up policy for just one payment if, for example, you inherit a large sum of money or wish to give a policy as a gift.

Endowment Policies. In contrast to other types of policies, endowment policies pay benefits to you while you are still alive. If you die before the maturity date, benefits are paid to your beneficiary. A policy that provides for "endowment at 65," for example, will pay the face value of the policy to you at age 65, or to your beneficiary if you die before you reach 65. You pay extremely high premiums under endowment policies because the insurance company must accumulate the full amount of your policy by the maturity date. You supply most of the face amount of the policy yourself, through the high premiums you pay. Endowment policies are therefore primarily geared toward forced savings for later years, rather than toward pure insurance, since other types of policies provide identical death protection for less money.

Life Insurance Companies. Life insurance is sold by two types of companies: *mutual life insurance* companies and *capital stock* companies.

Mutual life insurance companies are nonprofit corporations that are owned by the policyholders. These companies issue *participating* policies that pay you a *dividend*, or partial return of your premium. Under participating policies, premiums are usually higher than needed by the company and, as a result, the company is able to return a portion at the end of each year. Because the dividend represents a return of premium, it is not taxable as income to you.

Capital stock companies, on the other hand, are owned privately by stockholders, and their securities, or stocks, are listed on a national or regional stock exchange. Although some capital stock companies offer participating policies, they primarily write *nonparticipating* policies, under which you receive no dividends. Capital stock companies fix their premiums as accurately as possible to meet their expenses.

Comparisons between participating and nonparticipating policies are quite difficult because there are so many variables—length of ownership and changes in interest rates, for example. Any cost comparisons, of course, must use the *net cost* of participating policies (premium less dividend) over a period of years.

Other Life Insurance Considerations. The question of whether it is advisable to buy term insurance, which is cheaper, and invest the difference at a higher rate of interest, or buy whole life and combine insurance protection with an investment or savings feature is a debate that has continued for years. Neither approach can be unequivocally recommended, since each has its advantages and disadvantages. Neither must it be an either/or decision, because policies of term and whole life can be combined to increase protection while reducing premium costs. For example, a *family income* policy combines whole life with decreasing term insurance. The term portion is in effect for a specific period, usually 10, 15 or 20 years. If you die during this period, your family is provided with a monthly income for the remainder of the period. The face value of the whole life policy is payable either at the end of the monthly income period or, sometimes, in a lump sum at the beginning. The plan is geared toward providing a higher level of income when your family is growing.

The so-called *family policy* or *family plan* also combines whole life and term coverage. The family plan provides protection for the entire family in predetermined amounts in a single contract. For example, a family policy might provide for $5,000 of whole life on the wage-earning spouse, $2,000 in term for the spouse who is not a wage-earner, and $1,000 of term to age 21 for each child, including those not yet born.

For an increased premium, companies commonly provide several additional features. You can obtain a *double indemnity* rider, which means the policy pays twice the face amount if you die as a result of an accident. You can also obtain a *waiver of premium* rider so that if you become permanently disabled, your insurance will remain in force without having to pay any more premiums. Finally, you can purchase *guaranteed* insurability, which allows you to add insurance to your existing coverage without an additional medical examination.

Health Insurance

Almost daily, we hear reports on the soaring costs of medical care. The prospect of hospital rooms costing $100 and more per day, or of a relatively minor injury or illness resulting in medical expenses in the hundreds and perhaps the thousands of dollars, is a frightening one for all of us. These dramatic cost increases force almost everyone to purchase some form of health insurance protection. In fact, in recent years most personal health care bills have been paid by private health insurance, philanthropic groups, industry and the government.

Health insurance is designed to protect you and your family against two associated risks: the costs of medical care and loss of income due to disability. Private health insurance, however, is not the only type of health protection available to you. For example, you might be eligible for some of the following:

- Worker's compensation insurance if you're injured on the job.
- Social Security benefits if you become permanently disabled.
- Veteran's Administration payments if you are a war veteran who becomes totally disabled.
- Comprehensive health benefits at a very low rate if you are a government employee.
- Medicaid if your income is low enough to qualify
- Medical payments under your liability insurance or life insurance disability provisions.

There are five basic forms of health insurance:

1. Hospital expense insurance
2. Surgical expense insurance
3. Regular medical expense insurance
4. Major medical expense insurance
5. Disability income insurance

The basic health insurance plan combines hospital, regular medical and surgical expense insurance.

Hospital Expense Insurance. Blue Cross is a familiar example of this type. It provides two kinds of coverage. First, a *daily room-and-board benefit* pays for room and board and general nursing care in a semi-private room up to the number of days specified in your policy. If you want a private room, the plan pays a set amount toward its cost and you pay the balance. You pay for nonmedical services like a telephone and a television set. An *additional expense benefit* pays for other charges, like laboratory tests and x-rays taken in the hospital, anesthesia, drugs and medicines, use of the operating room and local ambulance service. Some hospital insurance contracts may require you to pay a deductible such as the first $50 or $100 of your hospital bill.

Surgical Expense Insurance. This insurance helps absorb the costs of surgeons' fees, whether incurred in the hospital or in a physician's office. Frequently, surgical expense policies list the benefits paid for many surgical operations. Since it is impractical to name every procedure, policies then state that benefits for procedures not listed will be consistent with comparable operations that are listed.

Regular Medical Expense Insurance. This generally covers costs of visits by or to a physician for services not involving surgery. Coverage may include extended home care, prescription drugs, diagnostic tests, and possibly dental work. Many people carry medical and surgical insurance in the form of the Blue Shield plan.

Major Medical. In addition to the basic protection plan afforded by hospital-surgical-medical coverage, people frequently secure back-up protection through major-medical insurance. This insurance is designed to protect you against heavy financial burdens that can result from a chronic illness or serious accident. It provides broader coverage than the basic plan, often paying, for example, costs of blood, drugs, and treatment for mental illness. This type of plan has two significant features. First, as with auto insurance, it comes with a deductible—often $100. The deductible makes it possible to obtain major medical at a lower rate, since the insurer does not have to pay a large number of small claims. Secondly, under major medical you pay a fixed percentage, usually 20 to 25 percent of all costs above the deductible up to the policy limits.

Basic hospital-surgical expense insurance and major medical may be combined into a single plan, often with a relatively low deductible of about $100. This form of insurance coverage is termed *comprehensive major medical expense insurance.*

Disability Income Insurance. This provides you and your family with continuing income if you are unable to work for an extended period. Depending upon your policy, you are guaranteed specified payments for either *partial* or *total disability*. Partial disability essentially means that you are unable to perform one or more of the basic duties connected with your work. Frequently, benefits for partial disability are payable only if the disability occurs apart from your job, since on-the-job disability is usually covered by worker's compensation insurance. Total disability is usually defined in policies as one or more of the following:

- Unable to perform the normal duties of your job for a year or longer.
- Unable to engage in any occupation you are fitted for by education, training or experience.
- Unable to engage in any gainful employment.

Some disability policies insure only the policyholder; others insure the policyholder's dependants. Disability income insurance almost always has a dollar amount or time limit on benefits and usually contains no provisions guaranteeing renewability. The two forms of disability insurance are sickness insurance and accident coverage. While you can buy each separately, they are most often combined in an "A and S" disability policy.

Group vs. Individual Health Insurance. There are two principal ways a family can get health insurance coverage: through a *group plan* or through an *individual or family policy*. Under group plans you may be covered immediately, or after a specified waiting period. Also, your protection generally ends when you leave the group, although it is often possible, at that time, to convert your insurance to an individual or family policy. Group insurance has certain advantages over individual or family plans. Premiums are lower because insurance companies save money in sales and administrative expenses by insuring the whole group under a single contract. Secondly, the employer or other group contract holder often pays part or all of the premiums. Thirdly, members of the group are eligible regardless of their physical condition. Finally, the individual's coverage cannot be cancelled unless the plan itself is terminated or unless he leaves the group.

Property and Personal Liability Insurance

Losses caused by fire are running more than $3 *billion* each year, and nearly 100 out of every 1,000 households are burglarized. The need for property insurance, the oldest form of insurance protection, is a fact of life for most property owners. Like most insurance, we buy it and hope we will never need to use it.

Property owners and renters can obtain insurance against losses in several ways. You can purchase different types of insurance protection separately or you can buy a package policy that protects you against several different perils. Even with a package policy, you can, for an extra premium, buy additional insurance for special needs.

Fire Insurance. Standard fire policies insure your home and its contents against fire and lightning. For an additional premium, you can obtain extended coverage to protect against wind damage, hail, smoke, explosion, riot, vehicles and aircraft. The standard fire policy also offers protection against certain kinds of losses that are incidental to fire. For example, if firemen break windows or use damaging chemicals on your belongings, your losses are covered.

What your fire insurance covers is spelled out in your policy. But you should know that to be covered by fire insurance, the fire must be *hostile* and *accidental.* Hostile means that the fire must burn in a place where it is not supposed to be and there must be visible flames. Lightning is included, however. Accidental means that the fire must start by accident or accidently get out of control. If you set a fire on purpose, for example, you will have no right to recover under the policy.

Several types of fires are not considered hostile—when the fire burns in a fireplace, oven, stove or furnace and you have started it, normally you are not covered. For example, if you mistakenly dispose of a valuable object in your incinerator, you are not protected since the fire occurred in its usual place.

Burglary, Robbery and Theft Insurance. *Burglary* means theft of property from your home by someone who breaks in by force. *Robbery* means the taking of your property, either inside or outside the home, by someone who uses violence. *Theft* is a catch-all term covering all forms of stealing.

Theft insurance often gives you blanket coverage for your belongings. You can also receive coverage on your property in two groups: furs and jewels in the first group and your other possessions in the second. If you have valuable items like rare books or paintings, or if you want increased coverage on money, stock, or other possessions, these can be listed and valued separately. You can also obtain a policy to cover all your possessions or special valuables against most of the risks you are likely to come up against. This type of policy is called a *floater*, and it protects your property not only at home but wherever you take or send it.

Liability Insurance. This protects you against losses from lawsuits brought for injuries suffered by visitors and damages caused to the property of others. Suppose, for example, that a visitor slips on your property and suffers a major injury, or suppose that while burning leaves, you damage your neighbor's property. Personal liability insurance provides two types of protection: *legal defense* and *payment of damages*. If the visitor sues you after slipping on your property, the insurance company will pay for your legal defense regardless of whether you are found to be at fault. Obviously, the insurance company will pay damages to the visitor only after it has been determined through settlement or by the courts that you are legally liable for the injury or damage.

Homeowner's and Renter's Insurance Packages. Buying separate policies may be best for owners with specialized property or those facing certain definite perils, but a package plan has several advantages. First, you usually have only one policy and one premium to worry about. Second, your property is insured against a wide variety of perils and you pay less than if you purchased separate policies. Familiar package policies are the *homeowner's* and *renter's* policies.

You can purchase a homeowner's policy if you own and occupy a one- or two-family residence. The policy protects both your house and additions to it, like attached garages. The policy also protects other structures, including storage sheds, guest houses, or detached garages; these are called *appurtenant structures*. Buildings used for commercial purposes or rented out (except garages) are not covered.

Under a homeowner's policy, all your household goods and personal belongings are covered. You receive protection whether the loss occurs at home or not.

Homeowner's policies specify certain exceptions and conditions under which losses will not be paid. For example, pets are not covered and protection for jewelry and furs is usually quite limited. The company may exclude theft of credit cards or coverage to boats when they are away from your premises. If you need extra protection not covered by your homeowner's policy, you can usually obtain it by paying an extra premium.

Homeowner's policies include an additional feature called *additional living expense*. The company pays for the increase in living expenses made necessary if damage to your home is so serious you must move out. For example, costs of hotels, motels and restaurant meals are covered. The company pays, up to a specified limit, only the difference between your expenses away from home and your regular living expenses.

There are three types of homeowner's coverage: the *basic homeowner's policy, broad homeowner's policy,* and the *comprehensive homeowner's policy.* The basic policy usually protects against the following perils: fire and lightning, wind and hail, explosion, riot, aircraft, vehicles, smoke, vandalism, theft, breakage of glass, and loss of property removed from premises endangered by fire or other perils. The broad homeowner's policy usually adds protection against falling objects, snow damage, partial or total building collapse, and water heating system breakdown. The comprehensive policy covers all perils except earthquake, landslide, floods of certain kinds, backing up of sewers, seepage, war, and nuclear radiation.

Many homeowner's policies contain *coinsurance* clauses. If you want to receive full payment for any partial damage or loss, you must insure your property for at least 80 percent of its replacement value; if you insure your property for less, and you suffer a partial loss, as coinsurer you must bear a proportionate amount of the loss, or are responsible for the difference between the amount of insurance you carry and 80 percent of the property's value. If, say, you own a cottage worth $25,000, you must purchase $20,000 in insurance, or 80 percent of the value of the cottage, to receive full payment for your partial loss (except for deductible amounts). It is always important to keep your level of protection at 80 percent of your property's value.

You should also be aware that many policies have *deductibles* under which you are obligated to pay for all losses up to a specified sum, usually $50 or $100.

Once you decide how much coverage you want on your home, the amounts of coverage for appurtenant structures, personal property and additional living expenses are automatically determined as a percentage of your total coverage. If you insure your $25,000 cottage for $20,000, or 80 percent, your coverage on appurtenant structures might be $2,000 (10 percent) of your total coverage; coverage for personal property might be $10,000 (50 percent of your total coverage) and $4,000 for additional living expenses (20 percent of your total coverage). Always be sure that these percentages (in dollars) are adequate coverage for you— for example, you may have personal property worth more than 50 percent of your total coverage, in which case you should be sure to obtain additional coverage.

Homeowner's policies also provide you with personal liability insurance as well as medical payment coverage. Under medical payment coverage, payments are made for injuries to other people caused by you, your family or your pets. This coverage is similar to personal liability except that it is designed for minor injuries—up to $500 per person, and payments are made regardless of who is at fault.

If you live in an apartment or rent a home, you can purchase *tenant's* or *renter's insurance*, which, like homeowner's insurance, is a package plan. Tenant's insurance, without insuring the building, protects the contents of your residence and personal possessions against the same perils as homeowner's insurance does, and it also provides for personal liability protection and medical payments to others.

Automobile Insurance

The enormous increase in the cost of automobile insurance is one good reason why all of us should know what this insurance protects us against and what types of policies are available on the market. Further, if you are an *uninsured* driver in Texas and you are involved in an accident, regardless of fault, you can lose your license if you are unable to come up with the money required by our financial responsibility law.

Basic automobile insurance coverage you should know about includes:

1. Liability, including bodily injury liability and property damage liability;
2. Medical payments, commonly called med pay;
3. Wage loss;
4. Substitute service, also called essential service;
5. Uninsured and underinsured motorist;
6. Collision;
7. Comprehensive.

Liability. This insurance protects you when you operate a car in a negligent (unreasonably risky) fashion and cause injury to other people or damage to their property (in other words, you are involved in a collision that results in damage of some kind, and *you* receive the ticket for negligent collision). *Bodily injury liability* applies when your car injures or kills pedestrians, passengers in other cars, or guests in your car. Bodily injury coverage will pay for your legal defense, regardless of who is ultimately found legally liable. Also, it will pay an agreed-upon settlement amount or award by the court, up to the limits stated in your policy. Amounts of coverage are usually written as 10/20, 25/50, or 100/300. The first number in each of these examples refers to the maximum amount, in thousands of dollars, your company will pay for injuries to any one person in any one accident. The second number is the maximum amount the company will pay, in thousands of dollars, for all injuries to all persons in any one accident.

Property Damage Liability. This insurance applies when your car damages another person's car or other property. It does *not* protect against damage to your car. You are covered as long as your car is driven by you, members of your immediate family, or others who drive your car with your permission. You and your family also are covered while driving someone else's car as long as you have the owner's permission. Property liability insurance pays for your legal defense, regardless of who is ultimately found legally liable, and it pays for damages, up to the policy limits, when you are found legally liable. Insurance agents refer to bodily injury coverage as "BI" and property damage liability as "PD."

Several states require drivers to carry liability insurance; Texas does not. Consequently, you can legally drive your car in Texas without liability insurance. If you are unlucky enough to be involved in an accident, however, and do not have insurance, Texas' financial responsibility statute requires you to post a bond of up to $25,000. Texas, like most states, requires you to post the bond immediately, regardless of whether you are eventually found liable for damages. Texas' financial responsibility requirements are set at 10/20/5. In other words, you must either carry insurance or be able to post a bond for up to $10,000 for each injury caused by your negligence, to an upper limit of $20,000 for total bodily injuries for all persons injured, and up to $5,000 for any property damage resulting from any one accident. If, under the law, you are unable to prove your ability to pay, your driver's license can be suspended for up to two years.

The Safety Responsibility Division of the Texas Department of Public Safety is responsible for administering our financial responsibility law. The practical effect of the law is to make auto liability insurance extremely advisable, even though Texas does not require it.

No-Fault Insurance. The underlying purpose of no-fault auto insurance is to do away with the hassle of determining liability except in the most serious cases. In states that have passed compulsory no-fault laws, *every* car must be insured. When a driver is injured in an accident, his own company pays, within limits, for his medical expenses and lost wages, regardless of who is at fault. Strict no-fault is not in effect in most states that have adopted the plan, since property damage and medical costs are not covered. Also, there are often limits on benefits, thus permitting injured parties the right to sue the person at fault. No-fault laws were originally designed to do away with the very expensive and time-consuming legal job of determining who is at fault, the seriousness of the injury, and how much should be paid to compensate victims for their injuries.

The "liability system" remains intact in Texas, which does not have a compulsory no-fault law. Texas does, however, have a voluntary form of no-fault protection called *personal injury protection coverage.* By law, automobile liability policies in Texas must include personal injury protection unless you specifically reject it. Coverage includes payment for medical expenses, benefits for loss of essential services (like an amount to hire a housekeeper if the housekeeper in your family is injured), and benefits for loss of income. These benefits are available to you and members of your household if they are injured in any automobile, and to *any* occupants of *your* automobile.

Medical Payments or "Med Pay." Med pay insurance is optional. It covers you and your passengers for medical expenses resulting from an accident in your car. It also covers you or your family if struck by a car while walking or if injured in someone else's car. The maximum benefits per person are specified in the policy.

Wage Loss and Substitute Service. These coverages are included in personal injury protection coverage. Compensation for loss of wages is limited in dollar amount and in the length of time you are eligible to receive payments. Substitute or essential services payments are payable for services you are unable to perform because of an injury and will cover the expense for these services for only a limited time.

Uninsured and Underinsured Motorist. Like personal injury protection, this coverage must be offered on auto liability policies in Texas unless you specifically reject the coverage in writing. *Uninsured* motorist coverage will pay for your injuries or damage to your auto or belongings in the auto if the injury or damage was caused by an uninsured motorist who is found to be at fault (legally liable). *Underinsured* motorist insurance covers you against a motorist who is insured but does not carry limits of liability equal to the uninsured/underinsured motorist coverage limits you have on your policy.

Collision Insurance. This covers damages to your car if it is in an accident, regardless of fault. The advisability of such coverage depends on several factors, including the age and value of your car. There is usually a deductible—often $100. The higher your deductible, the lower your premium.

Comprehensive Insurance. This optional coverage protects you from most other types of losses or damages to your automobile or its contents. For example, the policy will often cover losses caused by fire, theft, vandalism, earthquakes, explosions, falling objects, floods, hail, windstorms, and collisions with animals. As with collision insurance, the higher the deductible, the lower the premium.

Automobile Special Policies. All of the types of automobile insurance coverage described above are available in a standard policy called the *Family Automobile Policy.* Under this policy, you can receive duplicate medical payments; that is, you can collect from both your auto insurance and your medical insurance policies. The family policy uses a *split-limit* method to establish maximum amounts the company will pay for any one accident. For example, if your policy specifies 10/20/5, the company will pay $10,000 per person for injuries up to $20,000 for all personal injuries; and up to $5,000 for property damage.

Companies also offer a *Special Package Automobile Policy* which combines liability, personal injury protection, and uninsured/underinsured motorist coverage, with several other options available. The special policy is often less expensive than the family policy because it is available primarily to low-risk drivers. Also, med pay coverage is limited under the special policy, since it only pays medical expenses not covered by other policies.

Factors Affecting Insurance Cost. There are literally hundreds of factors that affect automobile insurance rating, which either increase or decrease your premiums. Some of the most prominent rating factors include:

1. *Age and sex.* The worst risk from the company's point of view is an unmarried male under age 25. Companies maintain that the best risk is a woman driver from age 30 to age 64.
2. *Use of the vehicle.* The more you drive your car, the higher your premiums are. Discounts are often available if you drive your car strictly for pleasure or if your drive to and from work is less than 10 miles. If you use your car mainly for business, your rates will probably be higher.
3. *Type of car.* As a general rule, the more expensive your car, the higher your rates are for collision and comprehensive coverage. Also, companies contend that sports cars and high-performance cars are more likely to be driven in a hazardous fashion, so they

often draw higher rates. Compact cars generally receive discounts, while high-performance cars may cost 50 percent more to insure.

4. *Driving or safety record.* Companies charge more to drivers who have, within the last few years, been involved in accidents or who have received traffic citations. Companies are also interested in the number of accidents you have had, regardless of who was at fault.

5. *Personal habits.* You may be eligible for a discount if you do not drink or if you are steadily employed.

If you are unable to obtain automobile insurance through the usual channels, you can make an application, through a licensed agent, to the Texas Automobile Insurance Plan. This plan will provide you automobile bodily injury and property damage coverage, with limits of liability sufficient to meet the requirements of the financial responsibility law. Uninsured/underinsured motorists insurance at the same limits must be provided, as well as personal injury protection coverage, unless you reject these forms of coverage in writing. Of course, this coverage will be considerably more expensive than is typical, since you are a high-risk driver.

You also have the option of dealing with insurance companies that specialize in covering drivers who are poorer risks. You will usually have to pay much higher premiums if you fall within this classification.

Shopping for Insurance

A prudent approach to the purchase of insurance may be summarized in three "knows": know your needs, know your agent, and know your company.

Know Your Needs

Only a careful analysis of your needs, and your financial ability to meet those needs, will enable you to shop for an appropriate policy. Even the best insurance agent is useless if *you* do not know your own needs. For example, the initial purchase of an inadequate or inappropriate life insurance policy may not become apparent until after some years have passed. During that time, your health may have deteriorated to the point where you are either uninsurable or insurable only at a greatly increased cost.

Switching life insurance policies is seldom advantageous, particularly in the case of whole life insurance. Cash surrender values on whole life insurance do not begin to accumulate substantially until after at least two or three years, because of the initial expense the company incurs in commissions and acquisition costs. Cash values build up much faster as the policy gets older. You will therefore usually lose money if you want to switch whole life policies. Also, after two years your life insurance policy will become *incontestable*. This means that with a few exceptions, the company cannot turn down a claim even if you made a misstatement on your application or concealed a material fact about your health.

Keep in mind that while a whole life policy *may* be best for you, you should arrive at this decision only after careful study. Commissions on term insurance are usually significantly lower than for whole life. For this reason, a few agents may recommend whole life because of its advantages for them rather than for you.

As with life insurance, knowing your needs when you purchase medical insurance is equally important. The spiraling costs of health care frighten us all. But never purchase medical insurance out of fear; purchase it only out of real need. Always be aware that more comprehensive benefits cost more. On the other hand, there are several considerations that may help reduce your medical insurance costs without sacrificing benefits.

• If you are covered under any group insurance program provided by an employer or employee organization, avoid duplicate coverage. Limit purchases of supplemental policies only to those needs not covered under your group plan. Also, remember that many group plans provide for family coverage. This may be less expensive than if you cover your family on an individual plan.

• When considering the purchase of additional insurance, first analyze your own financial ability to meet some medical expenses from sources other than insurance—perhaps from savings. If you are financially able to meet some expenses of medical care in this way, you may not need to purchase as much additional coverage.

● If you are not a member of a group insurance program and must bear the expenses of your medical insurance, the task of balancing your needs against your ability to pay is more difficult. In most cases, it is very expensive to be 100 percent insured. Initially, determine how much of the financial burden you can reasonably afford to bear. A policy providing for a $250, $500 or even $1,000 deductible is considerably less expensive than one providing for "first dollar" coverage.

● Many limited coverage policies are available which provide protection only for a particular disease, such as cancer. Although, this coverage may be desirable, you should be aware of the very limited benefits provided under such policies.

● Many insurance policies do not cover a medical condition existing prior to the purchase of the policy. When filling out an application for insurance, be careful to answer all questions relating to age and prior medical history fully and truthfully. Failure to do so may result in denial of your claim at some later date.

A few rules of thumb might make purchasing and maintaining your property insurance a little easier. With property insurance, maintaining the correct level of insurance is as important as purchasing the right amount of coverage in the first place. Since the value of your property will vary over time, and since you certainly want any claim handled as quickly as possible, make a periodic inventory. In fact, it is a good idea to photograph the contents of your house, particularly your valuables. This will ensure documentation for claims and federal income tax deductions.

Know the meaning of *actual cash value* when you buy property insurance, since the company generally pays only this amount in the event of a loss. Commonly called "ACV," actual cash value is determined by subtracting depreciation from the original purchase price. If you paid $500 several years ago for a television that is stolen, you won't receive $500 from the company. Instead, assuming the television depreciated in value to $200, that will be the maximum sum you can collect, regardless of your policy limits. Depreciation of your property is bound to occur unless the property is jewelry, paintings or other such valuables.

Property insurance only covers specific items owned by a specific person. If you move, a new policy must be written. Further, unless otherwise stated, the insurance company is only liable for the part owned by the insured. If you and a friend each own 50 percent of a boat that is destroyed while sitting in your garage, the company will pay you only for your 50 percent, not for the loss of the whole boat.

When shopping for auto insurance, keep in mind that if you buy other forms of insurance coverage from the same company, or have another car insured with the same company, you may get a sizable reduction in your premium. Like health insurance, when you buy collision or comprehensive, the more you pay in deductibles, the lower your premium will be. It is a good idea not to turn in claims for amounts just above your deductibles, since a high *frequency* of claims will raise your premiums and increase the possibility of your insurance being cancelled.

Auto insurance policies may be cancelled for a variety of reasons. Probably the most common are major accidents or a large number of traffic tickets. But it never makes sense to lie in order to get new coverage.

Know Your Agent

Because most of us are not insurance experts, we depend on the insurance agent a great deal for advice and guidance. And it is the potential influence of the agent on the insurance purchaser that has led to regulation of his activities by the State Board of Insurance. If you wish to verify the reputation of an agent, contact the Licensing Division of the State Board of Insurance (see Appendix A). Texas requires all insurance agents to be licensed by the State Board of Insurance. And an agent who writes casualty or fire insurance must obtain a separate license to write life insurance. Finally, some persons hold themselves out as insurance counselors, advisors or specialists. These persons may or may not be agents of an insurance company. Texas law states that an individual may use the title "life insurance counselor" or its equivalent only after passing a special examination that is more comprehensive than the examination required for an agent's license.

Know Your Company

The problem of choosing from among the 1,700 companies offering insurance in Texas is no simple one. Feel free to shop around. If you have any question as to the reputation of a particular company, several inexpensive and simple inquiries can be made.

All companies offering insurance policies in Texas must be licensed through the Company License Section of the State Board of Insurance (see Appendix A). If contacted by telephone or mail, the Section will verify the licensing of the company.

Local Better Business Bureaus may also be contacted for information concerning the company. Most public libraries contain the publications of Alfred M. Best Company, an independent insurance reporting service. *Best's Insurance Guide* lists and rates all insurance companies based on financial integrity or soundness. Also, the *Guide* contains information for each company on claims paid, premiums collected, investment income, and gains and losses. In addition, you might wish to consult the publications of the Consumers Union. Several *Consumer Reports*, published by the Union, rate insurance companies and review aspects of insurance coverage.

Watch out when you are dealing with mail-order insurance companies. A mail-order company may operate by mail because it is unable to get a license in Texas. And if the company is not licensed in Texas, the State Board of Insurance has no regulatory control over the company. The principal kinds of insurance sold by mail are health and accident policies, and life insurance policies. Because consumers have been misled by some mail-order insurers, the Federal Trade Commission prepared a booklet entitled *Mail-Order Insurance* (publication number N-01-1), which provides some pointers on spotting unscrupulous companies. You can receive a copy by writing the Federal Trade Commission, Washington, D.C., 20580. The Federal Trade Commission only has jurisdiction over mail-order insurance companies not licensed in Texas.

Unlawful Insurance Practices

Because an insurance policy is a contract like any other contract, you have a right to expect the insurance company to live up to its obligations. If the company refuses to pay a valid claim, it has breached its contract with you. When this occurs, you have the right to sue the company to compel it to meet its obligations.

Insurance companies ordinarily do not refuse to honor a claim unless their investigation leads them to the conclusion that their refusal is based on adequate legal grounds. Nevertheless, if you believe the company's conclusions are wrong and that they have paid you less than full value, or that the company's failure to pay a claim is unwarranted, you should complain to the company. If that does not work, follow procedures outlined in Chapter 10.

In addition to the legal rights based on your contract with the insurance company, Texas law protects consumers against several fraudulent and deceptive insurance practices. Fortunately, these practices are rare, not only because most insurance companies are reputable, but also because the industry is regulated by the State Board of Insurance.

Misrepresentations and false advertising of policies are prohibited. These might involve any of the following:

1. Misrepresentation with respect to the terms or benefits of any policy.
2. Misrepresentation about the dividends or share of the surplus to be received on a policy.
3. Misrepresentation as to the financial condition of an insurer.
4. Using any name or title for a policy which misrepresents its true contents.
5. Misrepresentations made to a policyholder by the agent to induce him to lapse, forfeit or surrender his insurance.

Other statements may also be considered misrepresentations if they (1) are untrue statements of a material fact; (2) fail to state a material fact; (3) are made in a manner that misleads a reasonable person to a false conclusion of a material fact; (4) misstate what the law is; or (5) fail to disclose any matter required by law to be disclosed.

Rebates are also prohibited. A rebate typically is an offer made to return part of an agent's commission to induce you to purchase insurance coverage. An agent might also offer an extra dividend or the return of part of your premium. Even indirect rebates are prohibited. For example, an agent cannot buy goods from an insurance applicant in order to get the applicant to purchase a policy from him.

All of us who are equal "risks" for the insurance company are entitled to be offered the same price for insurance. When a rebate is given, one policyholder is allowed an unfair advantage over others who are in a similar situation.

Another misleading (and unlawful) practice is called "twisting." By making incorrect or misleading comparisons of contracts, the agent attempts to convince you to cancel your insurance and buy the policy he sells. This practice frequently causes substantial losses, particularly if whole life insurance is cancelled.

Texas law provides for the penalizing of agents who perpetrate these forms of consumer abuse. The State Board of Insurance can suspend, revoke, or decline to renew the license of any agent who engages in misleading practices. In addition, penalties such as fines or imprisonment may be levied against agents who engage in the unlawful activities described in this section.

Texas law also prohibits lenders from coercing borrowers to buy insurance from a particular insurance company or agent. When you apply for a loan, the lender often will require you to obtain insurance before your loan is approved. A lender can require insurance. But a lender cannot dictate to you where you can obtain the insurance.

State Board of Insurance

The Insurance Commissioner and the State Board of Insurance have the major responsibility for regulating the insurance industry. The vast majority of states have an appointed commissioner who oversees insurance activities within the state. Texas, however, has a three-member Board appointed by the Governor. The Governor also selects one of the Board members to be Chairman.

The Insurance Commissioner is appointed by the three Board members. While the Board is responsible for supervising the work of the agency, the Commissioner has the day-to-day job of administering the law governing insurance practices.

The Commissioner and Board perform their functions through four major groups: Business Practices, Financial Monitoring, Research and Compliance, and Property and Casualty. Each group is headed by a Deputy Commissioner.

The Business Practices Group is particularly important to consumers because any complaints against insurance agents or companies should be filed with this Group. A complaint form (Figure 7-1, on the next page) is provided on request.

STATE BOARD OF INSURANCE
PRACTICES & CLAIMS SECTION
1110 SAN JACINTO
AUSTIN, TEXAS, 78786

IN RESPONSE TO YOUR RECENT REQUEST FOR ASSISTANCE WE ARE SENDING YOU OUR INSURANCE REPORT FORM. PLEASE COMPLETE THE FORM IN FULL AND RETURN IT TO THE ADDRESS ABOVE, ATTACHING ANY PERTINENT CORRESPONDENCE OR PAPERS. YOU WILL BE HEARING FROM US AS SOON AS WE RECEIVE THE COMPLETED FORM.

TYPE OF INSURANCE

COMPLAINANT_____ HEALTH___ LIFE___ AUTO___ FIRE___

ADDRESS_____ DISABILITY___ HOME OWNERS___ OTHER_____

_____ IF AUTO, GIVE TYPE OF CLAIM:

TELEPHONE NUMBER_____ LIABILITY___ PHYS. DAMAGE___ MED.PMTS.___

NAME OF INSURED (IF DIFFERENT FROM ABOVE) OTHER_____

_____ POLICY NUMBER_____

ADDRESS_____ DATE OF ISSUE_____

_____ DATE OF LOSS_____

NAME OF INSURANCE COMPANY AS SHOWN ON POLICY_____

HOME OFFICE ADDRESS OF CO._____

IS THIS THE ONLY COMPLAINT YOU HAVE FILED WITH THIS BOARD REGARDING THIS PARTICULAR MATTER?

YES____ NO____ IF "NO" PLEASE GIVE DETAILS_____

MAY WE SEND A COPY OF THIS COMPLETED FORM TO THE INSURANCE COMPANY IF NECESSARY?_____

PLEASE DESCRIBE YOUR PROBLEM BRIEFLY AND IN YOUR OWN WORDS. IF MORE SPACE IS NEEDED, PLEASE USE REVERSE SIDE.

_____
_____
_____
_____
_____
_____
_____
_____
_____
_____

_____   _____
DATE   YOUR SIGNATURE

REPORTED BY TELEPHONE_____ LETTER_____

Figure 7-1. *This complaint form should be filed with the Business Practices Group of the State Board of Insurance anytime you have a complaint against an insurance agent or an insurance company. A copy of this form will be sent to you on request.*

Public Utilities

From our earliest school days we are taught that monopolies are bad. Images of Teddy Roosevelt and his "trust busters" come to mind. Why then have our laws consciously decided that in so far as public utilities are concerned monopolies are good? The reason is economics. For each public utility—whether a telephone, electric, gas or water company— there is a tremendous investment required to deliver the service to customers. Pipes and wires must weave their way through cities and across miles of open countryside so none of us will be without services that are vital to our comfort, health and safety. If competition is allowed, the miles and miles of pipes and wires would be duplicated— the total investment doubled or tripled, depending on the number of competitors. The Texas Legislature has decided that expensive parallel sets of water and gas mains or parallel sets of telephone and electric poles should not be allowed so long as one company is able to provide satisfactory service at a reasonable rate.

The idea of a monopoly is distasteful because we know that open competition is the most effective, natural market control on the price and quality of goods and services. With competition, a business that charges exorbitant prices or sells inferior goods or services will lose customers to businesses with cheaper prices or better goods and services. Competitive businesses can grow and prosper only by keeping prices low, and the quality of goods and services high. Without competition, a business can deliver poor quality and charge whatever it pleases. This is particularly true of utilities because nearly all of us must have water, telephones, gas and electricity. When full market competition does not control the price and quality of utility service, government regulation is not only proper, it is essential.

Until 1975, the regulation of telephone, electric and water utilities was left to the cities and the utility companies themselves. Cities were provided almost no guidance for regulation under Texas laws, and rural areas were left without direct regulation. Consumers were not concerned about the situation as long as the service was good and the cost cheap.

It did not take long, however, for rates to climb.

Many city governments were unequipped to take on the expensive and complicated job of regulating the utilities. After all, utility regulation was but one of the thousands of concerns requiring the attention of city governments.

Utility rates continued to climb and before long, the public turned to the Legislature and demanded that something be done. The Legislature's response was the enactment of a law creating the Public Utility Commission of Texas.

Public Utility Commission of Texas (PUC)

The PUC is charged with representing the public interest while maintaining the financial integrity of Texas utility companies. Its job, in a nutshell, is to keep the price of telephone, electric and water utility services low enough to be fair to consumers yet high enough to allow a satisfactory profit for utility companies. The PUC is composed of three members, appointed by the Governor. The PUC has a staff comprised of six divisions working in two principal areas: rate evaluation, and regulation of rates and services.

Although gas rates and service are regulated by the Railroad Commission, the PUC has exclusive jurisdiction over the rates and services of electric, water and sewer utility companies in unincorporated areas (outside city limits) of Texas. Cities retained the power to regulate public utilities operating within their limits until September 1, 1977. On that date, many cities turned the reins over to the PUC while others decided to continue regulating utilities as they had in the past. The PUC does, however, have exclusive jurisdiction over all telephone utilities in Texas, regardless of where they operate.

Finally, the PUC has *no* regulatory jurisdiction over municipally owned utilities within city limits, or political subdivisions, such as municipal utility districts or political districts. That is, only the City of Houston can control the city-owned water company.

Texas Railroad Commission

The regulation of gas utilities in Texas is vested in the Railroad Commission or the cities in which gas utilities do business. The Railroad Commission is the oldest regulatory agency in Texas having been created by an amendment to the Texas Constitution in 1890. The three commissioners originally were appointed by the Governor. Railway industry leaders made such a political issue of this appointive process that today each member of the Commission is elected.

The Gas Utilities Division of the RRC regulates the transportation, distribution and sale of natural gas by *intrastate* (Texas) gas utility companies. This regulation includes the determination of fair and reasonable rates for natural gas and natural gas service.

The RRC has exclusive jurisdiction of gas companies regarding rate increases for rural areas. It also has jurisdiction over sales by gas utility companies to distribution companies serving incorporated areas like Houston or Dallas. The Commission also has appellate jurisdiction in gas utility matters whenever a city and a gas utility cannot agree upon a fair gas rate.

Table 8-1 indicates which utility services are regulated by which agencies or other governmental bodies.

Customer Rights

The PUC and RRC have issued rules which apply to those utility companies subject to their jurisdiction. These rules are the same as laws and must be obeyed by the companies.

Service Interruptions

The PUC and RRC require the utility companies they regulate to make all reasonable efforts to prevent interruptions of service. When it

Table 8-1
Who Regulates?

Utility Services	Government Agencies				
	PUC	RRC	PUC or Municipality	RRC or Municipality	Municipality
Inside city limits:					
Telephone	x				
Gas				x	
Electric			x		
Water			x		
Outside City limits:					
Telephone	x				
Gas		x			
Electric	x				
Water	x				
Municipal Utility Districts					x
City owned companies					x

PUC = Public Utility Commission of Texas
RRC = Texas Railroad Commission

is interrupted, all utilities must restore service as quickly as possible. Further, each utility regulated by the PUC or RRC is required to make plans for dealing with emergencies when failure occurs. These general rules ensure that a utility company's service is continuous and dependable.

Customer Relations

Since a utility company's rates are the main concern of its customers, the PUC and RRC require companies to post notices in their business offices informing the public that copies of rate schedules and rules relating to service are available for inspection. Upon request, these utility companies also are required to inform customers of their methods of reading meters.

If a customer complaint is filed with a utility company regulated by the PUC or RRC, the company is required to promptly investigate the complaint and advise the customer of the results.

Deferred Payment Plans

There are times when utility customers find themselves confronted with a particularly large utility bill that they are unable to pay in full. Although no utility is required to offer customers a deferred payment plan, the PUC and RRC encourage companies to do so. A deferred payment plan enables a customer to pay a particular month's bill in installments spread over several months.

If a utility company voluntarily decides to offer customers a deferred payment plan, it must follow certain rules. First, the deferred payment plan must promise the customer that service will not be cut off if the customer agrees to pay all current bills and pay the deferred bill in reasonable installments. In other words, once the company allows a customer to pay a deferred bill in installments, it cannot suddenly change its mind and cut off service.

Second, the installment payments under the deferred payment plan must be reasonable. If the payments are not reasonable then the purpose of having the bill deferred is defeated. In deciding what is "reasonable," the following factors must be taken into account by the utility company:

1. The amount of the delinquent account.
2. The customer's ability to pay.
3. The customer's payment history.
4. The length of time that the debt has been outstanding.
5. The reasons why the debt is outstanding.
6. Any other relevant factors concerning the circumstances of the customer (such as unexpected medical bills, etc.).

If you participate in a deferred payment plan you also have responsibilities. First, the company has the right to demand that you sign a statement promising not to dispute the amount of the bill being deferred. Second, the company can require you to pay a five percent penalty for late payment. And third, if you fail to make the payments for the amount and at the times specified in the deferred payment agreement, utility service can be cut off.

Refusal of Service

Utility companies have the right to refuse service to people who fail to abide by the companies' rules (which must be approved by the PUC or RRC), or who fail to abide by the rules adopted by the regulatory agencies.

Although individual company rules may vary, the following three grounds for refusal are considered valid by both the PUC and the RRC:

1. If your facilities are inadequate—faulty wiring or plumbing;
2. If you are indebted to another utility that provides the same service you are applying for (unless the bill is in dispute);
3. If you refuse to pay a deposit to a company that is authorized to charge customer deposits.

If a utility company refuses to give service on any of these grounds, you are not left without recourse. First, the utility company is required to tell you the specific reason for their refusal to provide service. Then, if you feel that the utility company has denied service unfairly, you may file a complaint with the appropriate agency.

The following are not valid reasons for refusing service. If you are refused service for any of these reasons, you should immediately file a complaint with either the PUC or the RRC:

1. Delinquency in payment for service by a previous occupant of the premises to be served.
2. Failure to pay for merchandise or charges for nonutility service purchased from the utility.
3. Failure to pay a bill to correct previous underbillings when the underbillings are (a) more than six months old, and (b) the fault of the utility company.
4. Violation of a company's rules about using unauthorized attachments or nonstandard equipment unless you have been notified of the violation and given a reasonable opportunity to comply with the rules.

5. Failure to pay a bill of another customer when you have signed as a guarantor on the other customer's account, unless the guarantee you gave was in writing and was the reason service was given to the other customer.
6. Failure to pay the bill of another customer at your address unless the customer's identity was changed in order to avoid or evade payment of a utility bill.

Some utility companies have used these grounds in order to collect what would otherwise be bad debts. If the customer who owes the money moves and cannot be located, there is no one from whom the utility company can collect its money except the new customer at the old customer's address. Demands of this sort are wrong. Imagine, for instance, that you are in a department store. You have just selected a suit of clothes, and as you start to pay for it the owner says "If you want this suit, you will have to pay for one just like it that was stolen yesterday." As ridiculous as this sounds, it is precisely what several of the "grounds for refusal" are saying. We must guard against abuses of this kind.

Discontinuance of Service

If your utility bill is unpaid and 20 days have passed since it was issued, the utility company may disconnect service unless other arrangements for payment have been made. You must be told, however, that your service will be disconnected. The notice of disconnection must be in writing and delivered to you at least *five* days before the service is cut off. The advance notice gives you an opportunity to pay the delinquent bill before you find yourself without the service.

A customer's failure or refusal to pay utility bills is not the only lawful reason for disconnecting service. Any of the following give the utility company the right to discontinue service:

1. Failure to comply with a deferred payment agreement.
2. Violation of a company's rules pertaining to the improper use of the utility service (such as using a "black box" on a telephone to avoid long distance toll charges).

3. Failing to comply with arrangements agreed to by you regarding deposits or a guarantee to pay another's bill.
4. Upon discovery of any dangerous condition relating to your service (such as a leaky gas pipe).
5. Tampering with a utility company's meter.

Again, some reasons used by some utility companies are not valid grounds for disconnecting a customer's service. The unlawful reasons for refusing service (listed in the section, "Refusal of Service" are also unlawful reasons for disconnecting service. Other unlawful reasons include:

1. Failure to pay for a different type or class of utility service unless the fee for the service is included on the same bill.
2. Failure to pay charges arising from an underbilling due to faulty metering, *unless* the meter has been tampered with *or unless* the underbilling charges are authorized by the PUC or RRC.
3. Failure to pay an estimated bill other than a bill that is given in accordance with an approved meter reading plan, *unless* the utility company's meter reader is unable to read the meter because of circumstances beyond his control.

If a utility company has valid reasons for disconnecting your meter, it can do so only if there are personnel on duty to collect payment on past due bills and to reconnect your service. In fact, the company must have these personnel on duty the day the service is disconnected and the following day. This rule ensures restoration of service as quickly as possible.

Finally, if a utility company finds it necessary to abandon a service area or a particular customer within a service area, it must give advance written notice. Utility companies do, on occasion, go out of business. The requirement of advance written notice gives the company's customers time to make alternative plans.

Utility Deposits

Utility companies charge deposits in order to protect themselves from customers who evade paying their bills. In most cases, we pay for utility service after it has been provided. The deposit helps assure the company that in exchange for providing service in advance it will have something to fall back on for payment.

Although customer deposits serve a useful purpose, some companies abuse their right to demand deposits. Some companies, for instance, collect more money in customer deposits than they will ever lose from customers who fail to pay.

The PUC and RRC have adopted rules on customer deposits to prevent abuses. A utility company can require a customer to establish credit by paying a deposit for service unless the customer is able to show one of the following:

1. You have been a customer of another utility company offering the same kind of service within the last two years *and* (a) your account is not delinquent; (b) during the last twelve months you did not have more than one occasion on which your bill was delinquent; *and* (c) you have never had your service disconnected for nonpayment.

2. You furnish *in writing* a satisfactory guarantee to secure payment of your utility bills.

3. You demonstrate a good credit rating that may be easily verified by the utility company.

If your service has been disconnected because of nonpayment of bills, then you must pay all delinquent bills before the company is required to reconnect your utility service. Once your service is reconnected, the company can require you to pay a deposit until you have re-established credit in one of the ways set forth above.

Utility companies give senior citizens a special exemption. If you are 65 years of age or older, you cannot be required to pay a deposit if, during the past two years, you have paid all outstanding utility bills. The fact that some bills may have been paid late does not matter. The only question is whether all bills are paid at the time you apply for new service.

Amount of Deposit

If a utility company does require you to pay a deposit, then that deposit cannot exceed an amount equal to one sixth of your estimated annual billings. For example, if your average monthly bill for electricity is estimated at $30, then your estimated annual billing will be $360 or $30 × 12 months. One sixth of your estimated annual bill would be $60. Therefore, the company could not charge you more than a $60 deposit.

When a utility company obtains a deposit, it must pay interest on that deposit at the rate of six percent annually. The only exception is when the deposit is refunded within 30 days after it is paid. Assuming that your deposit is $60, then your annual interest payment from the utility would be 6 percent × $60 or $3.60.

If you want to receive annual interest payments from the company, you must ask for them; otherwise, your deposit and the accrued interest will be returned to you when your deposit is refunded or credited to your account.

Refund of Deposit

A utility company is under a duty to refund a customer's deposit (plus accrued interest) when the customer's service is disconnected. Of course, if you have an unpaid balance at the time your service is disconnected, the deposit can be applied to the balance. The difference would be refunded to you.

The company must also refund a customer's deposit when the customer has established a good credit history by paying bills promptly during the preceeding 12-month period. In fact, even if you were delinquent in paying any two months' bills, the company must refund your deposit if at the end of the 12-month period your account is current.

Customer Billing

As previously discussed, the amount of utility bills is the overriding concern for most customers. Although occasionally we have been successful in reducing the amount some utility companies charge us, such as in the Southwestern Bell case, it seems likely that utility bills will be difficult to reduce in the future.

Although we cannot put a stop to all increases in utility rates, we can demand that the bills be accurately computed. It is one thing to pay high rates for utility service; it is another to be asked to pay even more because of a billing error.

Utility companies are required to include enough information on their bills to enable us to determine whether they are accurate.

Telephone Bills. Bills for telephone service are normally sent out monthly. These bills must contain:

1. The period of time covered by the bill.
2. A clear listing of all charges due and payable.
3. Itemized toll (long distance) statements.
4. A breakdown of local service charges (when requested in writing by the customer).

Telephone companies also are required to respect privacy be sending all bills in envelopes.

Electricity and Water Bills. Bills for electrical and water service must be sent out monthly unless the PUC authorizes another billing period. Also, the bills must be mailed as quickly as possible after meters are read. An electricity or water bill must contain all of the following information when applicable:

1. If the meter is read by the company, the date and reading of the meter at the beginning and end of the billing period must be shown.
2. The applicable rate schedule title or code (so the customer can be sure the correct rate schedule is being used).
3. The total service charge if billed separately from fuel costs (electricity bills only).
4. The monthly fuel charge if authorized, together with a factor by which it is computed (electricity bills only).
5. The total amount due for electricity or water used.
6. The date by which the customer must pay the bill in order to avoid a penalty.
7. The total amount due after addition of any penalty for nonpayment within a designated period.
8. A distinct marking to identify estimated bills.
9. Any conversions from meter reading units to billing units, or any other calculations to determine billing units from recording or other devices, or any other factors used in determining the bill.

All of this information must be arranged on the bill in such a way that a customer can easily compute the charges for utility service. The PUC forbids utility companies to use terms like "gross bill" or "net bill" which lead customers to believe they are being offered a discount for prompt payment. If terms like these are used, there must in fact be a discount off the normal charge for the utility service. The terms cannot be used when a penalty is added for nonpayment within a specified period.

Gas Bills. Bills for gas service must also be sent out monthly unless the RRC authorizes a different billing period. Companies also are under a duty to send the bill out as promptly as possible after customers' meters are read.

A gas bill must contain the following information:

1. If the meter is read by the company, the date and reading of the meter at the beginning and end of the period for which the bill is issued.
2. The number and kind of units billed.
3. The total amount of the base bill.
4. The total amount of any adjustments to the base bill and the amount of any adjustments per billing unit.
5. The date by which the customer must pay the bill to get a "prompt payment discount."
6. The total amount due before and after any discount for prompt payment within a designated billing period.
7. A distinct marking to identify an estimated bill.

As you can see, the RRC allows gas utility companies to use the terms "net" and "gross" to indicate discounts for "prompt payment." However, a customer is not really offered a discount because a bill is paid within the 15 days allowed. Instead, the customer is assessed a penalty for failing to pay the bill when due. The net bill is actually the normal charge for the service. The gross bill is the normal charge plus a penalty for late payment. Therefore, even though these terms are still in use among gas utility companies, do not be misled as to their real meaning.

Estimated Bills

Many utility companies, particularly in large cities, periodically estimate a customer's meter reading in order to save the time and money required to read each customer's meter every month. The meters that are to be estimated normally are staggered so that no one meter is estimated for several consecutive months. These estimated readings are then used to prepare the customer's bill.

Well-trained meter readers are surprisingly accurate at estimating meter readings. Nevertheless, the potential for inaccurate billing is considerably greater than when meters are actually read. For this reason, utility companies must state on the bill whether or not it is an estimate.

Actual meter readings must be taken at least once every six months. This requirement means that you will have the opportunity to correct inaccurate bills twice a year.

Water and electricity companies must notify you each month if your bill is about to be estimated to give you the opportunity to read it yourself. For gas utilities, you must be notified when (1) the meter reader is unable to get to your meter for two consecutive months, or (2) when meters are not otherwise read. The required procedure calls for the utility company to send you a post card requesting that you read the meter and return the card to the company. If the post card is not received by the company in time for billing, then your bill may be estimated.

Disputed Bills

If there is any dispute as to the amount of a bill from a utility company, the company must investigate the complaint immediately and send you the results of the investigation.

Citizen Participation

In recent years we have seen a trend among utility consumers of questioning—sometimes loudly—applications for rate increases by utility companies. When the Attorney General's office took Southwestern Bell Telephone Company to court over what was thought to be an exorbitant rate increase, the office received hundreds of letters from citizens throughout Texas encouraging it to keep up the fight. City council chambers seem to be more active now when utility rate increases are proposed; the Public Utility Commission has had its chambers filled to capacity during hearings on rate increases.

Citizens are realizing that although a utility company may have a right to *ask* for higher rates it does not have the right to always obtain the requested rates. Rates and quality of service are inextricably woven together in the law. As more people realize this, demands for better service in exchange for higher rates are becoming louder.

Few in the Attorney General's Consumer Protection Division will forget the day when the residents of Greenwood Village subdivision in Houston "stormed" the Houston office. These citizens felt they were getting the run-around by several local and state government agencies. They decided to make their demands more vocal. More than 20 Greenwood residents, accompanied by most of the news media in Houston, marched into the office and demanded immediate action.

Their complaints were valid. The division decided to try to help. By the time the case was finished, the division had been to court countless times; the manager of the utility company spent several nights in jail for contempt of court; and the Public Utility Commission's attention was directed to the problem. As it turned out, the first order issued by the Commission was issued on behalf of the residents of Greenwood Village and neighboring subdivisions.

If enough citizens show their concern over rates or services, a proper investigatory process can be set in motion. The process is not swift. But the process can work if we put our energy into making it work.

The best advice for consumers who have problems with utility companies is to get involved. Request action from the government agencies that are responsible. It is your right *and* your duty.

Business
Opportunities:
Legal or Illegal?

Illegal operations by business opportunity promoters result in the loss of thousands of dollars annually in Texas. Many consumers are attracted to business opportunity promotions as a way to supplement the continually diminishing purchasing power of their paychecks. Retired people enlist in business opportunity schemes because they are unable to live comfortably on fixed incomes. And, unfortunately, hundreds of people lose everything because of some unscrupulous promoters.

Legitimate business opportunity promotions do exist. Thousands of Texans have pulled themselves from financial ruin by seizing good opportunities. But because of many who have not been so lucky—because of those who have been unable to distinguish a good opportunity from a fraud—the subject deserves special attention.

This chapter explores several common types of business opportunity promotions that have appeared in Texas in recent years. An attempt will be made to alert you to some methods of operation which seem to be used by most con men who run fraudulent promotions. And, finally, an approach for evaluating a business opportunity promotion is provided to help you spot fraudulent promotions before they have a chance to harm you.

Types of Business Opportunities

Business opportunity promotions tend to fall into one of three categories: investments, services and distributorships.

Investments

An investment business opportunity means what the name says: You are asked to invest your money into someone else's business.

A typical example of an investment business opportunity is found in a series of cases filed by the Attorney General's Consumer Protection Division against a group of "Schedule D" oil promoters and a land syndication company.

"Schedule D" Investments. "Schedule D" is a provision in the Internal Revenue Code that allows a tax break for people who invest in certain types of oil or gas drilling companies. In 1976, the division began to receive complaints from many consumers who felt they were deceived by some of the promoters. Shortly after the investigation began, a former employee of a company came to the Consumer Protection Division's office with a tape recording of a standard telephone sales pitch made by one of the company's principal promoters as a training aide. The recording was incriminating enough and was introduced as evidence in the prosecution of this company.

This sales pitch was an extreme example of hard sell. The consumer involved did not send the check; the company was successfully prosecuted and is now out of business. Nevertheless, many consumers lost their investments before the unlawful practices were stopped.

Investment business opportunities are unique in that the investor is not required to do anything other than invest money. You are forced to rely *entirely* on someone else's ability and honesty. For this reason, most investments of this sort are considered "securities" which means they are regulated by the State Securities Board. The Board requires companies subject to its jurisdiction to register before they can make investment offers to Texas residents. Several "Schedule D" companies, however, attempted to avoid this requirement by selling only to people who live outside of Texas. Although their attempts ultimately failed, the fact that they were not registered in Texas enabled the promoters to forestall prosecution. Thus, more consumers were damaged than might otherwise have been the case.

Land Syndication. Several years ago, land syndication was an extremely popular type of investment business opportunity. Land values were on the rise, and money was fairly easy to come by. The idea behind land syndication basically is this: Because an individual may not have enough money to purchase a piece of property, a group of individuals join together, pool their resources, and buy the land. Through syndication, investors with smaller amounts of money are able to participate in a business that formerly was only for the very rich.

Because of its popularity, the land syndication business began to attract people who were out for a quick profit. And, it was not long before the Attorney General's Consumer Protection Division became involved.

In one case, the parent company was involved in approximately 25 land syndication partnerships. Each syndication owned at least one tract of expensive, commercial real estate in Harris or Montgomery counties. Most of the tracts of land were worth several hundred thousand dollars or more.

The mechanics of a land syndication are relatively simple. A land syndicator (the organizer) will locate a piece of property, which in his judgment, can be purchased and then sold a short time later for a good profit. The syndicator then offers a limited number of prospective investors the opportunity to buy into the partnership. The money raised through the syndication process (investor buy-ins) is used to make a down payment on the property and put the partnership in a position to resell. If the property is resold quickly, the debt on the property is retired, and the profits remaining are divided among the partners, depending on the amount each invested. Problems develop for syndications when the property cannot be resold quickly at a profit. This case illustrates these problems.

After the 25 partnerships had been formed and 25 separate tracts of land purchased (on credit), the money market suddenly grew tight. New buyers for the properties could not be found. As time passed, payments on the notes used to finance the purchase of the tracts came due. To satisfy the demands of the various creditors of the partnerships, the owner of the company began to take funds from one partnership to pay the debts of another. Like falling dominoes, the time soon came when there were no other partnerships from which money could be taken. Because most of the investors were told they would only have to pay their pro-rata share of the down payment and perhaps a few interest payments, they were understandably upset when they learned they would have to continue pouring money into the partnership in order to keep the property.

Some of the property was saved, and a few investors got their money back. Most, however, lost their investments. Again, the necessity of relying on the ability and honesty of someone else to make your money work demands great caution.

Employment

We are all anxious to find ways to improve the quality of our lives. Many times this means looking for a better job. Because of this, when we see advertisements promising employment opportunities that provide higher pay, better working conditions, or more responsible positions, they are very attractive. Once again, however, when consumers are willing to pay money for a needed service, con men are prepared to enter the picture.

One of the most tragic cases ever handled by the Attorney General's Consumer Protection Division involved a Houston-based company.

The company was an advance fee résumé service. This meant that for a certain sum of money paid in advance, the company provided you with a "professionally prepared" résumé and a mailing list of prospective employers. By contacting these employers and sending a copy of your résumé, you were supposedly able to get a job offer from at least 1 or 2 of the 500 companies on the mailing list. The fee for this service was $395.

Had the company described its service as it is described here, customers would have been able to evaluate the service. But instead of telling customers the truth, the company promised its customers that they would definitely get a job in Alaska or overseas working in the skilled trades at an annual wage of $45,000 to $65,000.

More than 700 customers paid money to this company. Yet, after months of investigation, neither the Consumer Protection Division nor the company itself could ever prove that anyone got a job. The company folded; the owners left the jurisdiction; and no one got their money back.

This was but one of several advance fee résumé services to move into Texas several years ago. Most are now out of business.

The employment opportunity cases illustrate an important fact of modern business life of which all consumers should be aware. Because of the tremendous numbers of people living in Texas cities, it is quite possible for a business to operate for several years without having a repeat customer. When a business must have repeat customers to survive, its customers do not usually need to worry about consumer protection. But in the large, urban areas, this important check on business activities is often missing. For this reason, most consumer complaints and consumer protection problems are found in the cities.

Distributors, Manufacturing and Production

Another main category of business opportunities are those which offer consumers distributorships, or manufacturing or production rights.

In the 1960s and early 1970s, distributorship frauds swept the country. Most of the fraudulent schemes were pyramid sales operations which have already been discussed in Chapter 1. Aside from pyramid sales schemes, however, there are other problems frequently experienced by consumers who invest money in distributorships.

A distributorship gives a person the right to distribute a product or service of another. People buy the right to distribute in anticipation of the profits to be made from sales to either retail outlets or directly to the public. The cost of investing in a distributorship is usually quite high. Therefore, if the product or service to be sold through the distributorship does not have a proven market, the risk of loss is considerable. The experience of a Waco investor in a distributorship illustrates the harm that can be done when a promoter is less than truthful about prospects for success.

In 1974, a woman was approached by a company salesman. Among other things, this person was told that no special ability or aptitude was required to become a successful distributor of the company's products; that she would encounter no difficulty in selling the products; that the company's distributors are uniformly successful; and that all distributors enjoy a substantial income. Unfortunately, each of these representations proved to be deceptive. Nevertheless, relying on the representations, she invested nearly $11,000 in a distributorship.

Unlike many others, this story has a happy ending. A lawsuit was filed against the company. The jury agreed that the woman had been deceived by the company and had suffered damages as a result. She recovered all of her money.

In more recent times, a new type of distributorship has come to Texas. This variation of the old scheme contemplates the sale of "rights to manufacture" a product. The items to be manufactured normally are small decorator items. The necessary equipment takes little space so that the work can be done in a garage or spare room.

In 1976, several companies began selling "rights to manufacture" to Texas consumers. Most of these companies were from California. Legal problems were not new to many of the principals behind the companies. One company sold the right to manufacture coasters from beer cans. Along with the right to manufacture the product, an investor received necessary equipment and supplies. The key feature that made the scheme attractive to Texas consumers was a provision in the contract which stated that the company would "buy-back" all of the production. In other words, investors would not be concerned with selling the coasters once they were made. Many consumers lost thousands of dollars because the buy-back promise turned out to be empty.

The fraudulent use of a buy-back gimmick can be very subtle. For instance, some companies will buy the production of initial investors in order to get good recommendations. Then, these recommendations are used to sell additional manufacturing positions to other investors. Once a large number of people have purchased manufacturing positions, the company will go out of business leaving everyone high and dry.

Another technique used by fraudulent companies that sell rights to manufacture is to fly investors to the home office for special training in the manufacturing process. Although the training offered generally is legitimate, the purpose of the trip, from the company's viewpoint, is to provide the investors with a feeling of confidence in the company.

Another of these companies sold investors the right to manufacture plastic wall decorations. After an investor signed the contract and paid the purchase price (cashier's checks only), the company flew the investor to Los Angeles for training and orientation. The training site was also the place where previously manufactured products were stored. As the investors participated in the training course, they saw stacks of the items they were learning to manufacture being moved out of the facility, presumably for shipment to retailers, and new stacks of manufactured items being brought in. All of this movement in the warehouse area gave several investors the impression that the items were selling very well. A joint investigation by the Consumer Protection Division and the Los Angeles District Attorney's Office later revealed that the products were simply being moved from one warehouse to another and then back again in order to give the *appearance* of sales activity.

Methods of Operation

The "MO" (method of operation) of fraudulent business opportunity schemes frequently fits a pattern. Although all of the following elements may not be present in each scheme, many of them will be. One word of caution: The fact that a business opportunity plan has one of these elements in its program does not necessarily mean that the program is a fraud. Instead, it should only serve to put you on guard— to make you aware that the program needs to be studied *very* carefully before you invest in it.

Large Initial Investments

All fraudulent business opportunity schemes investigated by the Attorney General's Consumer Protection Division have required investors to pay large sums of money as a condition to participating in the program. The reason for this in a fraudulent scheme is that the promoters know they will not be in business for long; therefore, they must make all their money on the front end. A corollary to the large initial investment is the company's promise that you will be paid back— either through the buy-back gimmick or some type of return on your investment—but your pay back will be *deferred* until sometime in the future.

Unproven Business

Although all promoters claim that their business opportunity is a sure thing, few of the fraudulent operators can point to a successful track record. Frequently, they will point with pride to the success of competing companies as if their success is a barometer of how well your investment will do. The fact is, another company's success or failure has little or nothing to do with the prospects for *your* investment. Most business opportunity schemes fail, not because the ideas are poor, but because the people running the companies leave a lot to be desired.

Transient Salesmen

Beware of business opportunities which are negotiated in motel rooms. Transient salesmen can be an indication that a company is rapidly expanding in order to collect as much money on the front end as possible. Although it is not a fixed rule, often the more transient the salesmen are, the more transient the businesses will be.

Pressure to Invest

Any legitimate business opportunity can wait a few days to allow investors time to think over the potential risks. This is especially true when thousands of dollars are on the line. But most fraudulent schemes are sold as if there is no tomorrow. "We're only offering a limited number of these positions" or "I've got to close out my sales by tonight" are typical statements used by promoters to get you to sign up quickly. The reason for the pressure is that most fraudulent promoters know better than to give prospective investors the time to think about or discuss the investment opportunity. Just a few moments of reflection may save you from financial disaster.

Suggestions on Self-Defense

Ways to protect yourself against fraudulent promoters of business opportunities include:

1. If is sounds too good to be true, it is! Listen to what you are told by the pomoter. If it does not make sense to you when you hear it, it certainly will not make sense later when you try to sell it.
2. Carefully check all references given to you. If none are given, demand them. And remember, references can be staged just like other misrepresentations. If telephone numbers are supplied, take

the time to call information to make sure the number given is
listed the way it should be in the telephone book. It may just be the
promoter's home phone with a friend standing by.

3. Do some market research on the idea you are asked to invest in.
The public library is a tremendous source of information.

4. Check with regulatory agencies in your area *and* in the state where
the home office is located. Also check with the local Better
Business Bureau or the Chamber of Commerce. In short, try to
develop a profile of the company through independent third parties.

5. Demand that *all* material representations about the opportunity
or the company be in writing and, preferably, signed by the
salesman. If a promoter is not willing to reduce what is said to
writing, it means he does not want to face it again. Also, by getting all representations in writing, you will have evidence if the
scheme is fraudulent.

6. If you are asked to invest a substantial amount, consult with your
lawyer and banker to get their advice on the investment.
Sometimes people who are not directly connected with a transaction are better able to see the flaws in it.

Probably the best suggestion on self-defense is to approach business
opportunities conservatively. If you find that the company exhibits any
of the characteristics described in this chapter, or, if the company has
other characteristics that disturb you, then be wary.

If you are to make money, you must spend money. There is an ele-
ment of risk in every investment. Deciding whether to invest in a
business opportunity is a balancing act—you must balance that which
you hope to achieve against the amount that you stand to lose. Great
risks do, on occasion, bring great rewards. But you must remember, the
reason the risks are great is because so many fail. Thorough investigation and careful thought are your best defenses against losing money
to a fraudulent business opportunity scheme.

How to Get Action on Your Complaint

Things will go wrong. Regardless of the care taken to avoid consumer problems, there will be occasions when we find ourselves confronted with a transaction gone sour. When things go wrong, we now have several effective and efficient remedies available. Before turning to these remedies, however, we should first exhaust the "informal" or non-adversary techniques by which many consumer complaints are settled.

Effective Consumer Complaints

The first informal or friendly technique by which a consumer complaint may be resolved is to do the obvious: complain to the business. Complaints made directly to the business involved in the transaction can be very effective because most businesses are extremely concerned about what customers think of them. Word-of-mouth advertising is the most effective way to promote a business. When the words coming from consumers' mouths are negative, it is also the most effective way to destroy a business. For this reason, most businesses have an acute interest in seeing that their customers are satisfied.

Consumer complaints are most effective when a few, simple rules are observed.

1. Put the Complaint in Writing. Many consumers who have legitimate complaints about a consumer transaction are tempted to pick up the telephone, call the business and verbally demolish the first person who has the misfortune to answer the call. Unfortunately, aside from causing unnecessary ill feelings between the consumer and the business, such calls accomplish very little. Even if the call is a friendly one, it still may accomplish little. Since there is no written record of the information conveyed by the call, the possibility for misunderstanding and delay is considerable. A written complaint will provide a permanent reference to ensure that the complaint-handling procedure of the business is responsive to your individual problem.

Several of the legal remedies discussed in this chapter require you to give advance written notice of complaints to businesses. The purpose of the requirement is to afford the business an opportunity to settle the complaint without a lawsuit. When written notice is required, a consumer who fails to give notice will find the available legal remedies substantially curtailed. Therefore, by making all consumer complaints in writing, valuable legal rights are preserved.

2. Make the Complaint Complete. A consumer complaint is only as valuable as the quality of the information it provides to the business. Most businesses require certain basic information in order to process consumer complaints. If the information is not provided in the first writing, valuable time will be consumed in follow-up letters.

Some consumer transactions will generate more than one complaint. That is, a consumer may have a legitimate complaint not only about the performance of the product or service, but also about the salesperson's conduct, excessive charges, or any number of other facets of the transaction. Unless all complaints are set forth in the first letter to the business, the force of the complaints will be diminished considerably. You may even run the risk of being labeled a "chronic complainer" by the business. Once personnel who handle complaints develop this attitude toward you, the chances for an amicable settlement are diminished.

A consumer complaint should contain the following information in order to be complete:

- The consumer's name, address and telephone number;
- The date and place of purchase;
- The name of the salesperson;

- A description of the product, including any model or other identifying numbers;
- A copy of any receipt, order, invoice or contract used in the transaction;
- A detailed statement of the complaint;
- A statement of the corrective action the consumer wants the business to take to resolve the problem.

When making a written complaint to a business, strive to make the letter businesslike. The letter should not reflect a threatening attitude. Most businesses encourage legitimate consumer complaints because they know that unsatisfied customers will not be repeat customers. No one, however, likes to be threatened.

You should always keep a copy of any letters sent to businesses. While this obviously is true of the first letter in which the complaint is stated, it is equally true of any follow-up letters concerning the complaint. Should the complaint not be settled as a result of your direct contact with the business, the legal remedies which must then be pursued will require a completely documented history of the dealings between you and the business.

Finally, all complaint letters should be sent by certified mail. This involves additional expense, but it provides good, reliable evidence that the letter was received by the business.

3. Direct the Complaint to the Proper Person. The larger the business, the more important this suggestion becomes. Like all large organizations, large businesses have specific personnel who are hired to do very specific jobs. In some businesses, there are complaint departments whose only job is to process consumer complaints. If your complaint is sent to the wrong person, the time required for the business to reroute the letter to the correct person will cause a delay in handling the complaint. The easiest way to determine the proper person to contact is to call the business and ask. A five-minute phone call may save a five-day delay.

There are times when we cannot determine who should handle the complaint. In these cases, the letter should be directed to the president of the company. This suggestion may be helpful in two ways: First, the president will know the proper person to handle the complaint. This will ensure that the complaint is routed within the organization as quickly as possible. Second, the complaint letter will then have a "buck-slip" (internal memorandum) from the office of the president requesting that the complaint be handled. Sometimes, lower level employees will act more promptly when they think the president of their organization is interested in the progress of their work.

If you have difficulty getting the name of a person to whom a complaint should be sent, there are some reference sources that may be of assistance.

If a business is conducting its affairs under an "assumed name," that is, a name other than that of the true owner, then the County Clerk's Office should have the owner's name on file in the assumed name records.

The local Chamber of Commerce or Better Business Bureau may be able to provide the owner's name if it cannot be located in the County Clerk's files. Also, if the business is a member of a trade association, such as the Independent Garagemen's Association, the local association office should be able to provide the information.

If the business is a corporation, and the information is not otherwise available, reference books in the local library often contain the names of the owners, officers and directors of larger corporations. Books such as *Standard and Poor's Register of Corporations, Directors, and Executives, Moody's Industrial Manual* and the *Standard Directory of Advertisers* should be consulted.

4. Suggest Corrective Action. You should always make a clear and concise statement of the corrective action requested from the business. Because a tremendous range of options are open to a business when a consumer complains, such as refund, replacement, or repair, it is not uncommon for a business to spend its time and resources approaching a consumer problem from one angle, only to learn later that the corrective action being taken is not what the consumer wants. By advising the business at the outset of the corrective action that will be acceptable, wasted effort and delay will be avoided.

The complaint letter is your best approach. Again, if later correspondence makes demands not previously stated, the business is likely to turn a deaf ear. Therefore, it is particularly important that the initial complaint letter set forth all demands that will be made during the informal stages of the complaint process. A consumer can rarely, with success, escalate the demands once the complaint process has begun.

Complain to the Company or Manufacturer

If a complaint to the local business fails to resolve the problem, then you should consider going to the next level—the company's head-quarters or the manufacturer.

There are times when a local business will ignore or fail to act on a consumer complaint. The pressures of day-to-day problems may delay action on consumer complaints. Consumer complaints should be af-forded the highest priority by all businesses; and, when they are not, consumers should feel justified in complaining to a "higher authority."

When local businesses are part of a chain, then the higher authority to which a consumer should turn is the headquarters. The name of the individual to contact as well as the address should be available at the local store. In fact, many businesses have a toll-free consumer "hotline" maintained expressly for the purpose of assuring prompt ac-tion on complaints.

If the product involved in the transaction was manufactured by someone other than the local business, then a complaint directed to the manufacturer often is effective. Manufacturers are extremely con-cerned with the manner in which retailers sell products because their sales volume is contingent on the goodwill generated by the local business. Manufacturers can also influence local businesses who wish to retain the right to sell their products.

Complain to Trade Organizations

All of us like to be well-liked by our peers. This characteristic of human nature is worthy of consideration when we have a legitimate complaint on which no action is taken by a local business.

Many businesses dealing in common products or services belong to trade organizations or associations. For instance, most automobile dealers belong to the Texas Automobile Dealers Association (TADA); many automobile repair shops belong to the Independent Garagemen's Association (IGA); and homebuilders often belong to local "home-builders' associations." Because the members of these organizations are concerned about their reputations with the membership, a complaint directed to the business' trade organization may help expedite action.

Legitimate business organizations have a vested interest in seeing that consumers are satisfied with the performance of member businesses. Consider, for example, what has happened to the used car industry.

For many years, used car dealers showed inadequate concern for the unlawful practices of a small number of their "colleagues." Because the practices of a few went unchecked, the industry as a whole developed problems.

An atmosphere of distrust is not conducive to good business. The tragic fact is that the atmosphere of distrust which hangs over many businesses is created by only a handful of law-breakers—a few people with little concern as to whether consumer complaints are satisfied.

An increasing number of businesses—manufacturers, large chains and local stores—are realizing that other businesses' unanswered consumer complaints may eventually come to rest on their own doorsteps. This enlightened attitude has opened another avenue for the resolution of consumer complaints.

Complain to Better Business Bureaus

Better Business Bureaus were created to accomplish what the name implies: make businesses better. One of the principal functions of most Better Business Bureaus is to process consumer complaints.

Aside from the peer influence created when a local Bureau contacts a member and requests action on a complaint, the Better Business Bureau's mere interest in the transaction can aid in its resolution. Many Better Business Bureaus report to consumers who inquire on the record of local businesses in responding to consumer complaints. These reports are issued to consumers who are looking for a place to do business, but who want to be sure that the business has a good reputation. Consequently, a business that fails to respond to an inquiry from the Bureau about a consumer transaction runs the risk of losing future customers because of an unfavorable report.

Most Bureaus take their responsibilities seriously and will work hard on behalf of consumers who file complaints with them. (A list of the Better Business Bureaus in Texas is included at the end of this chapter.)

Complain to Government Agencies

There will be occasions when your complaint to a business, and even to the business' trade organization, will go unanswered or unsatisfied. In these situations, you should consider making a formal complaint to an appropriate government agency.

Local Government Agencies. In larger cities, it is not uncommon for the city or county government to have a department of consumer affairs that handles consumer complaints. There are a number of consumer fraud divisions in various district attorneys' offices throughout the state. Because these offices are located near the businesses complained against, they frequently are able to use their influence to help solve disputes. These offices are listed in the telephone directory along with other local government agencies.

State Government Agencies. Local government agencies generally are geared to handle complaints relating to a wide range of consumer transactions. One local office frequently will take complaints on anything from insurance to consumer credit. State agencies, on the other hand, have limited jurisdiction and will not take complaints unless the transaction complained of comes under the particular laws enforced by that agency. Therefore, it is important to have some knowledge of the function of various state agencies to ensure that a complaint will be directed to the proper official (see Appendix A).

The success rate in handling complaints and the enthusiasm with which complaints are investigated varies from agency to agency. If the leadership of the agency is consumer oriented, then the agency's personnel may be expected to reflect that attitude and pursue consumer complaints accordingly. If the leadership of the agency is not consumer oriented, then the consumer who complains to that agency is not likely to be satisfied. The important point to remember is that the apathy (or enthusiasm) of one state agency should not be translated to mean that all state agencies are the same way.

Most state agencies require you to file a complaint in writing if you want the agency to take action. This enables the agency to make sure that your complaint is valid and not just a spur-of-the-moment release of anger. All state agencies receive their share of "crank calls." It would be very unfair for an agency to subject a business to the time and expense required to answer official inquiries only to learn later that the consumer's complaint was not made in good faith.

The following paragraphs briefly describe the functions of the Attorney General's Consumer Protection Division to illustrate the approach most state agencies can take to consumer complaints.

Consumer (or business) complaints relating to all types of fraud or deception in Texas are handled by the Attorney General's Consumer Protection Division. As with most state agencies, the Attorney General's authority is limited to enforcing particular laws. In the case of the Attorney General, he has the authority to investigate and prosecute violations of the Texas Consumer Protection Act. Part of this authority includes the power to file lawsuits against people who engage in deceptive trade practices in order to recover, for individual consumers, money or property that has been lost as a result of the unlawful activities of the business.

As with many state agencies, there is an important limitation on the Attorney General's power to file lawsuits for consumers. All lawsuits filed must be "in the public interest." This phrase means that more than one consumer must be affected by the unlawful conduct of the business. If the complaint grows out of an isolated transaction, then the Attorney General's Office is limited to trying to settle the complaint through mediation.

All complaints filed with the Attorney General must be in writing. Upon request, a complaint form, as shown in Figure 10-1, will be furnished.

There are some helpful hints in filling out the complaint form that should be kept in mind. First, make sure the form is filled out completely. All of the information requested is essential, otherwise, it would not be requested. If the information is not provided initially, the processing of your complaint will be delayed until complete information is obtained.

The second suggestion involves what *not* to write on the complaint form. For instance, slanderous remarks about the business or its personnel should be left out. Remember, the primary purpose of filing a complaint with the Attorney General's Office is to *negotiate* a complaint so it may be settled. If a business sees itself being slandered by a consumer, its desire to negotiate any type of settlement will be lessened. Also, unimportant details should be omitted. The race, hair color or

(Text continued on page 184)

Attorney General of Texas

CONSUMER PROTECTION AND ANTITRUST DIVISION
(DIVISION DE PROTECCION PARA EL CONSUMIDOR y ANTICARTEL)

OFFICES

1315 Lavaca
P.O. Box 12548
Austin, Texas 78711
512/475-3288

701 Commerce, Suite 200
Dallas, Texas 75202
214/742-8944

723 Main, Suite 610
Houston, Texas 77002
713/228-0701

806 Broadway, Room 312
Lubbock, Texas 79401
806/747-5238

4824 Alberta Ave., Suite 160
El Paso, Texas 79905
915/533-3484

4313 N. 10th, Suite F
McAllen, Texas 78501
512/682-4547

200 Main Plaza, Suite 400
San Antonio, Texas 78205
512/224-1007

IMPORTANT

This complaint form is provided to you with the understanding that this office may conduct investigations to determine if a business or person is in violation of the Texas Deceptive Trade Practices-Consumer Protection Act. (Subchapter E, Chapter 17, Texas Business and Commerce Code.) The filing of this complaint may or may not result in legal action against a merchant or business. We strongly recommend that you consult with your private attorney to determine your legal rights and remedies in this matter. IT IS VERY IMPORTANT THAT YOU FILL OUT THIS FORM COMPLETELY AND RETURN TO OFFICE NEAREST YOU. PLEASE USE TYPEWRITER OR PRINT IN BLACK INK.

IMPORTANTE

Este blanco para queja del consumidor se le facilita de acuerdo con lo siguiente: Esta oficina tendrá el derecho de investigar su queja para determinar si acaso el negocio o individuo ha violado la ley. No todas las quejas resultarán en demanda judicial y litigación. Le sugerimos que consulte con su abogado particular respecto a sus derechos y recursos legales. ES MUY IMPORTANTE QUE UD. LLENE ESTE BLANCO EN TOTAL Y LO PRESENTE A LA OFICINA MÁS CERCANA. POR FAVOR, ESCRIBA CON LETRA DE IMPRENTA CON TINTA NEGRA O MÁQUINA DE ESCRIBIR.

Your Name _____ (Su nombre)

Street Address _____ (Su dirección)

City and Zip Code _____ (Ciudad y zona postal)

Home Telephone _____
(Número de teléfono de su residencia)

Business Telephone _____
(Número de teléfono de su trabajo)

Date of Transaction _____
(Fecha que se hizo el trato o contrato)

Type of product or service _____
(¿Que compró?)

Have you complained to the company? _____
(¿Se ha quejado con la compañía?)

If so, when? _____
(¿Cuándo?)

Your attorney's name and address, if applicable (El nombre
y la dirección de su abogado, si acaso consulto con alguno) _____

Name of firm or person complained of
(Persona o compañía de quién se queja)

Address _____ (Dirección)

City, State and Zip Code _____
(Ciudad, estado, zona postal)

Telephone _____ (Número de teléfono)

Did you sign a contract? _____
(¿Firmó un contrato?)

If so, attach a copy
(Si firmó, mande una copia)

Name of finance company, if any _____

_____
(¿Fue la compra financiada, y por quién?)

Figure 10-1. All consumer complaints to the Attorney General must be in writing. Upon request, the Attorney General's office will send you a complaint form like this one. (Note the Attorney General's local offices and phone numbers.)

dress of a salesperson has little to do with whether your complaint is valid. The space provided on the form for answers is limited for a purpose: to encourage you to reduce your complaint to the essential facts.

Federal Government Agencies. You may also file a complaint with federal government agencies when you have a complaint which falls within their jurisdiction. With some exceptions, most federal agencies can accept complaints only if the company does business in more than one state—the company must be involved in *interstate* commerce as opposed to *intrastate* commerce.

The principal federal agencies with which you may need to file complaints are listed in Appendix B.

Small Claims Court

Small Claims Court is exactly what the name says: a judicial forum for the resolution of disputes involving small amounts of money.

The concept of a system of courts designed to provide inexpensive and uncomplicated justice for small civil disputes is not new. As early as 1518, a statute was passed creating a small debts court for the city of London.

The first small claims court in the United States was established in 1913 by the Municipal Court of Cleveland. It was called the "conciliation branch court" and its purpose was to settle claims involving $35 or less. Massachusetts established the first statewide system of small claims courts in 1920, followed by California in 1921. Then, in 1953, the Texas Legislature enacted a statute calling for the creation of small claims courts in this state.

From the beginning, the traditional formal pleadings characteristic of other courts were dispensed with and replaced by a simplified procedure for stating claims that was fair, effective, inexpensive and expeditious.

In the last 25 years, small claims courts have drawn criticism as being collection agencies for professional creditors. And yet, according to the National Institute for Consumer Justice, the same speedy and effective justice is available for consumer plaintiffs as for business plaintiffs.

Small claims courts are "plaintiff's courts." In Los Angeles, a study found that 86 percent of the consumer-plaintiffs prevailed in litigation that proceeded to hearing. In Philadelphia, almost two thirds of the consumer-plaintiffs' cases resulted in judgment for the plaintiff or a settlement. When cases voluntarily dismissed are excluded, the figure increases to just short of 90 percent. Although there are no figures available for the percentage of cases won by consumer-plaintiffs in Texas, there is no evidence that the result in Texas would be any different than that of any other state.

In spite of occasional criticism, there are several positive features of small claims courts that make them worthy of consideration.

The best features of these courts are the low cost of bringing a lawsuit, and the short amount of time it takes to prosecute a case from start to finish. Nationwide it is unusual for a consumer-plaintiff to pay more than seven dollars for filing a claim in small claims court and obtaining service of process on the defendant. And, although trial by jury costs an additional three dollars in Texas, it is seldom requested.

Justice is speedy in small claims court. If you can provide the correct name of the defendant and can supply an accurate address and time of day when the defendant can be served with a copy of the complaint, the case is generally heard within 30 days. To illustrate the efficiency of small claims court, consider Harris County. In this, the largest county in the state, there are 16 justices of the peace who are located in precincts throughout the county. In addition to their other duties, they hold small claims court once or twice a week. From three to ten cases usually are heard during each session. There is no backlog of cases in Harris County Small Claims Courts. In fact, it is unusual for a consumer to have to attend court more than twice: once to file the complaint, and once for the trial.

Another good thing about small claims court is the trial. The procedure is simple, the atmosphere is informal. Attorneys are not needed. In fact, in some courts they are practically barred. It is not unusual for the judges to question witnesses and parties on both sides in order to determine the truth.

Small claims courts are neighborhood courts. In most places, there is a small claims court near the consumer's residence or the place of business where the transaction occurred.

Finally, and most importantly, the clerks of Texas small claims courts provide assistance to consumers who need to use their courts.

The biggest drawback to small claims court is that far too few consumers know about them or how to use them. As the following sections show, if you have a small claim, small claims court is the place to be!

Suing in Small Claims Court

A claim suitable for small claims court must not exceed $500.

Anyone can be sued in small claims court so long as that person or business is present in the State of Texas or makes his home in the state. Also, if a person has property in the state, he may be sued, but only for an amount equal to the value of the property.

If these two general requirements are met, then the following steps should be taken to file a small claims lawsuit.

1. Select the Right Court. In most cases, you must sue in the *county precinct* where the person being sued resides. There are exceptions to this rule. For instance, if the person being sued (the defendant) has contracted to perform work or services in a county other than the one in which he resides, then he may be sued in that county. If there are any doubts on the correct court, ask the clerk at the small claims court nearest you.

2. File a Claim. After the right court has been selected, it is necessary to file a claim in that court. The filing of the claim starts the procedures in motion. Generally, your claim is a sworn factual statement of the transaction as well as the amount of and reasons for your damages. The claim must contain the following elements:

- Complete name and address of the person being sued (the *defendant*);
- Complete name and address of the person filing the suit (the consumer-*plaintiff*);
- Amount sued for;
- Basis of claim to amount sued for;
- Any amounts owed by the consumer-plaintiff to the defendant.

Figure 10-2 illustrates the proper form for a small claims court complaint.

3. Pay the required fees. After your claim has been prepared, you must pay all fees before your lawsuit can proceed. Normally, no more than three fees will be involved in any case. The first is the *filing fee*

```
  THE STATE OF TEXAS          X   IN THE JUSTICE COURT, Precinct No. 1
                              X
  COUNTY OF HARRIS            X   HARRIS COUNTY, TEXAS

  TO THE HONORABLE_____, Justice of the Peace:

  PLAINTIFF:  John Consumer, 1500 Branard St., Houston, Texas

  DEFENDANT:  ABC Merchant, Inc., 100 Travis St., Houston, Texas
                  Registered Agent:  Jim Merchant
                  Registered Address:  100 Travis St., Houston, Texas.

  CAUSE OF ACTION:  On January 2, 1978, I purchased a set of
  knives and forks from ABC Merchant, Inc.  The salesperson for
  ABC, Mr. James Jones, told me that the knives and forks were
  stainless steel, so I purchased the set for $52.00 cash.

      After a few weeks of use, the knives and forks began
  to corrode.  It was then that I discovered that they are made
  of aluminum, not stainless steel like I was told.

      ABC Merchant, Inc. has refused to give me my money back
  even though I have complained to the store several times.

  TOTAL AMOUNT SUED FOR:  $52.00 plus court costs as allowed by
  the Consumer Protection Act.

                              John Consumer
                              ─────────────────────
                              PLAINTIFF

      BEFORE ME, the undersigned notary public in and for said
  County, on this day personally appeared JOHN CONSUMER, who,
  after having been by me duly cautioned and sworn, did state
  to me upon his oath that the facts stated in this claim are
  true and correct.

      SUBSCRIBED AND SWORN this 1st day of April,
  19__, witness to which my hand and seal of office.

                              Marline Limaugh
                              ─────────────────────────
                              NOTARY PUBLIC IN AND FOR HARRIS
                              COUNTY, TEXAS.
```

Figure 10-2. *This is the proper form for a small claims court complaint. It must contain the name and address of the defendant and the plaintiff, the amount sued for, the basis of the claim, and any amounts the plaintiff owes the defendant.*

which covers the cost of processing the claim. This fee is approximately $3. Next, you will have to pay a *service fee* in order to have a copy of your claim served on the defendant by the sheriff or constable. This usually costs approximately $4 for each defendant you are suing. Finally, in the unlikely event you want a jury trial you must pay a *jury fee* of approximately $3.

4. Get ready for trial. Once the fees have been paid to the court, the judge will order a citation to be served on the defendant and a trial date will be set, usually several weeks after the defendant is served. Although the court normally notifies you of the trial date, it is a good idea to check with the clerk to be certain.

To prepare, you should carefully go over all testimony and documents needed to prove the facts alleged in your claim. The fact that you have written a complaint does not mean you have proved your case. Each fact alleged in your complaint must be proved at the trial through testimony by you or someone who witnessed the transaction, or by documents. If you relied on an advertisement, bring it to court. If you signed a contract, or were given a receipt for payment, bring that to court. In short, bring all papers or records that are in any way connected to the transaction. Then, once you are in court, be prepared to present your case to the judge in an orderly and understandable fashion.

It may be helpful to outline your case before going to court. The outline should be in chronological order. A chronological outline will keep you from skipping around when testifying before the judge, and will help avoid confusion concerning the nature of your complaint.

5. Trial in Small Claims Court. The trial in a small claims court consists of the presentation of evidence (testimony and documents) by the plaintiff and the defendant. Both sides have the right to test each other's evidence by asking questions of all witnesses. It is not unusual for the judge to question witnesses to ensure that all facts are before the court.

Frequently, the defendant will fail to show up for trial. When this happens, the judge may still require you to present evidence of your claim to make sure the claim is valid.

Once all evidence has been presented, the judge will enter an appropriate judgment either for or against you.

6. Collecting the Judgment. A judgment is simply an enforceable right to be paid money by the defendant. If the defendant refuses to pay you the amount of the judgment then you must ask the judge to order the sheriff or constable to *execute* the judgment by seizing a sufficient amount of the defendant's money or property to satisfy the judgment. You must allow the defendant 20 days to pay the judgment voluntarily.

If the sheriff or constable is unsuccessful in finding money or property of the defendant, then you may record your judgment in the County Clerk's Office. This process is called *abstracting* a judgment. Once your judgment is recorded, you will have a lien on any real estate owned by the defendant in the county in which the judgment is filed. This "judgment lien" will make it difficult for the defendant to sell his property until the judgment is paid off.

7. Appeal. The judge may rule against you. That is, he may decide that your claim is not valid, or, that even though the facts you present are true, there is no legal recourse. If you are dissatisfied with the judge's decision, there is a right of appeal from the small claims court. It should be noted that the defendant also has this right.

The right of appeal has one limitation: The amount involved in the dispute must be over $20.

If either party decides to appeal the judge's decision, a *Notice of Appeal* must be filed in the county court within ten days after the decision of the small claims court. Then, because the procedure in county court is quite complicated, you should get an attorney.

Suing a Business

If a business is intended by a consumer to be the defendant in small claims court, there are some special rules which must be followed if a valid judgment against the business is to be obtained.

It makes sense that if we are suing someone, we should identify that person accurately in the documents filed with the court to make sure that the person knows he is the target of a lawsuit. For this reason, a lawsuit filed against *John* Jones will be meaningless if *James* Jones is the wrongdoer. Even if the judge enters a judgment, it will not be enforceable against James unless he is foolish enough to show up for trial and participate in the proceedings.

Businesses have "legal" names. If a lawsuit against a business is to be successful, the claim filed with the court must identify the business by its correct legal name.

The correct legal name of a *sole proprietorship* (a business owned and operated by one person) is the individual owner's name followed by "d/b/a" (doing business as) and the name under which the business is operated. For example, if Joe Merchant owns ABC Meat Market, then the correct name to use on the claim form would be, "Joe Merchant, d/b/a ABC Meat Market."

If the business is a *partnership* (a business with two or more owners) then you name either or both of the partners individually in your claim form, followed by "d/b/a" and the name of the partnership. An example of this would be, "Joe Merchant and Jane Seller, d/b/a ABC Meat Market."

If the business is a *corporation*, the claim form must show the full corporate name. The law requires corporations to identify themselves by using "Company" or "Incorporated" (or their abbreviations) after the business name. Therefore, your claim against a corporation would be shown on the claim form as a suit against "ABC Meat Market, Inc." or "ABC Meat Market, Co." depending on the designation chosen by the corporation.

When you sue an individual or a partnership, a copy of your claim form is served on the individual or individuals named as defendant(s). This is not true with a corporation. Because a corporation is not a flesh and blood person, but rather a "legal entity," corporations are required to name an individual upon whom legal papers can be served. This person is called a "registered agent." The name and address of a corporation's registered agent can be discovered by contacting the Corporation Division of the Texas Secretary of State's Office in Austin.

Hiring A Lawyer

When calls and letters to a business go unanswered; when the Better Business Bureau and trade associations are unable to help; when the government is unable to respond with a satisfactory resolution of your dispute; and, when your claim is too large to be handled by small claims court, then you should consider hiring an attorney.

The function of an attorney is to stand in your shoes and, by his or her specialized knowledge and training, move your complaint through the courts until the dispute is settled.

Attorneys are expensive. And, even though several Texas statutes now require a defendant to pay attorney's fees to a consumer who wins the lawsuit, there still may be considerable time and expense involved in contracting with an attorney to handle your case.

Also, as with any other profession or business, the quality of attorneys varies. Unless your attorney is qualified and diligent, the time and expense you invest may be of little help in settling the problem.

Choosing a Lawyer

Most people require the services of an attorney only a handful of times during their lives. Most of us hire attorneys to help with major purchases such as homes; plan our estates so loved ones will be provided for after we are gone; and, dissolve an unsuccessful marriage. Aside from these major events, however, few consumers ever retain the services of an attorney. And, even fewer consumers use the services of an attorney on a regular basis. Because of our infrequent experience with attorneys, many of us do not know where to turn for legal assistance.

A lawsuit is a major event in anyone's life. Since an attorney's abilities frequently mean the difference between success or failure, the selection of an attorney may be the most critical choice you make in the process of resolving a complaint.

There are several methods by which you can select an attorney. The only reliable method, however, is by recommendation. If you decide to hire a lawyer to pursue your claim, go to your friends, to your banker, to your business associates, and to others whose judgment you trust and ask for the name of a good attorney. This method of selection is not foolproof, but it is the best method available.

When you have the name of a good, consumer attorney, visit him and discuss your case. Two things should result from this conference: (1) the attorney's professional evaluation of your claim; and (2) your personal evaluation of the attorney.

Attorneys are paid for their advice. They are trained to evaluate the financial merits of a claim. Therefore, if the attorney counsels against pursuing the claim, the advice should be seriously considered. Of equal importance, however, is your personal evaluation of the attorney. Remember, it is *your* claim. You must have confidence in the advocate you select.

If you do not know a lawyer, and if you do not know anyone who is able to recommend a good lawyer, then there is another way to find a competent attorney. Call the Lawyer Referral Service. Most county bar associations maintain lists of lawyers who practice consumer law. The referral provides no recommendation as to quality, but it does give you the names of attorneys who have indicated a desire to take consumer clients.

Legal Aid Services. Because of low income, many consumers are unable to hire attorneys, even though all other avenues of assistance have failed to resolve the complaint. Legal aid services across the nation have been formed to provide limited assistance to consumers whose financial condition would otherwise prevent them from benefitting from our system of justice.

If you have a low income and are unable to hire a private attorney when you need one, contact the legal aid service nearest you. Although there are strict rules as to who may use legal aid as well as what types of cases legal aid can participate in, a consumer with no other alternative should feel free to consult such services. A directory of legal aid services in Texas is included at the end of this chapter.

Legal Remedies

Legal remedies are those things which you can obtain or recover in a lawsuit against someone who has harmed you. There are two main types of remedies: money (damages), and court orders requiring the person you sue to do or not to do certain things.

Money

Most lawsuits are filed because the plaintiff believes that the defendant has caused some sort of financial harm. For example, if you purchased an automobile because of a representation that it had been driven 10,000 miles, and you later discover that the dealer rolled back the odometer from 100,000 miles, you would want to sue the dealer for the difference in value between what you were told you were getting (a 10,000 mile car) and what you actually purchased (a 100,000 mile car). That difference in value is called *damages*.

Many consumer complaints involve sums of money that are too small to justify going to court. Lawsuits are expensive. For this reason, several of the consumer protection statutes in Texas allow consumers to sue for more than just the amount they have been damaged. (See Table 10-1.) For instance, the Consumer Protection Act (which prohibits all forms of misrepresentation) allows consumers to sue for *three times* their actual damages plus attorney's fees and court costs. Similarly, when your complaint involves a dispute with your landlord over a security deposit which you can prove has been unlawfully withheld, you can sue the landlord for $100 plus three times the amount of the deposit wrongfully withheld and attorney's fees.

The idea behind these statutes is to give people who have suffered the ability to do something about it—in court. In other words, these statutes attempt to open the courthouse doors to consumers with small claims.

Court Orders

The other principal legal remedy available to consumers is to ask the court for an order which commands the defendant to do something or not to do something. Most of the time these orders are known as *injunctions*.

Consumers frequently sue for injunctive relief in debt collection cases. To illustrate, assume that you are being called by a debt collector 24 hours a day. Because of this, you may have suffered damages that you want to sue for, and you want the debt collector ordered to stop making the calls. In this case, you would sue for damages and an injuction. If you win, the court will issue an order requiring the debt collector to stop making the calls.

Injunctions may also be obtained to protect others. For instance, if a business is using an unlawful "bait-and-switch" scheme in selling its products, you may want a court order to stop the practice so other con-

Table 10-1
Legal Remedies Available
if You File a Lawsuit

Basis of Lawsuit	Chapter Reference	Remedies Available
Breach of contract	1, 2, 3, 9	Actual damages
Breach of warranty (goods, services, real estate)	1, 2, 4	3 times actual damages Attorney's fees Court costs
Debt collection	6	Actual damages Attorney's fees Court costs
Door to door sales	1	Contract voided Actual damages Attorney's fees Court costs
Landlord-tenant (security deposits)	4	$100 plus 3 times amount of deposit withheld Attorney's fees
Landlord-tenant (interruption of utilities, exclusion of tenant, unlawful seizure of tenant's property)	4	Recover possession or terminate lease Actual damages plus One month's rent Attorney's fees (*less* any delinquent rentals)
Misrepresentation, Unconscionability	1, 2, 3, 4, 5, 7, 9	3 times actual damages Attorney's fees Court costs

sumers will not be harmed. In this case, you are acting as a "private attorney general," doing for the public at large what the Attorney General normally would do. Consumer protection laws encourage lawsuits of this sort because everyone realizes that we will never have—and would never want—a government so large that it could protect everyone. Instead, we give private citizens the power to protect themselves and each other with the government doing as it properly should.

This discussion of legal remedies is simplistic. Literally hundreds of volumes have been written on the intricacies of the law of remedies. The purpose here is simply to point out the general nature and availability of these remedies.

Because of recent changes in the law, cases that could not have gone to court several years ago are now being resolved in courts. A consumer's chances of winning what is rightfully his are better today than ever before.

Better Business Bureaus in Texas

Joe E. Felton, Exec. Vice Pres.
BBB of Abilene, Inc.
P.O. Box 3275
325 Hickory Street
Abilene, TX 79604
(915) 677-8071

Marilyn Boone, General Manager
BBB of the Golden Spread
518 Amarillo Building
Amarillo, TX 79101
(806) 374-3735

H.W. Dunlop, Pres. & Gen. Mgr.
BBB of Austin, Inc.
American Bank Tower, Suite 720
Austin, TX 78701
(512) 476-6943

Mary Ann Kittell, Exec. Vice Pres.
BBB of Southeast Texas, Inc.
Goodhue Building, Suite 405
Beaumont, TX 77701
(703) 835-5348

LeRoy Balmain, Exec. Dir.
BBB of Brazos Valley, Inc.
307 Varisco Building
Bryan, TX 77801
(713) 823-8148

C.W. Vetters, Manager
BBB of Corpus Christi, Inc.
403 North Shoreline Drive
Suite 100
Corpus Christi, TX 78401
(512) 888-5555

James H. Kolter, President
BBB of Metro Dallas, Inc.
1511 Bryan Street
Dallas, TX 75201
(214) 747-8891

Jerome A. Morris, Gen. Mgr.
BBB of El Paso, Inc.
2501 North Mesa Street
Suite 301
El Paso, TX 79902
(915) 544-2420

Charles O. Unfried, President
BBB of Fort Worth & Tarrant
  County
709 Sinclair Building
106 West 5th Street
Fort Worth, TX 76102
(817) 332-7585

Richard McLain, President
BBB of Metropolitan Houston, Inc.
1212 Main Street
Houston, TX 77002

Malcolm T. Cleland, President
BBB of the South Plains, Inc.
915 Texas Avenue
P.O. Box 1178
Lubbock, TX 79408
(806) 763-0459

Allen L. Beatty, President
BBB of the Permian Basin, Inc.
Air Terminal Building
P.O. Box 6006
Midland, TX 79701
(915) 563-1880

Leo W. Taylor, President
BBB of San Antonio, Inc.
406 West Market Street
Suite 301
San Antonio, TX 78205
(512) 225-5833

Rosemary Taylor, President
BBB of Waco, Inc.
608 New Road
P.O. Box 7203
Waco, TX 76710

Directory of Legal Aid Services

Abilene Legal Services
221 Oak Street
Abilene, TX 79602
(915) 677-8591

Amarillo Legal Services
Box 12032
1715 American National Bank Bldg.
Amarillo, TX 79105
(806) 373-6808

Bexar County Legal Aid Association*
203 West Nueva Street
San Antonio, TX 78207
(512) 227-0111

Dallas Legal Services Foundation,
  Inc.*
912 Commerce Street, #202
Dallas, TX 75202
(214) 742-1631

El Paso Legal Assistance Society
1st National Bldg., Suite 1500
109 N. Oregon
El Paso, TX 79901
(915) 544-3022

Galveston Legal Foundation
503 National Hotel Bldg.
2221 Market Street
Galveston, TX 77550
(713) 763-0381

Gulf Coast Legal Foundation*
609 Fannin Bldg., Suite 1909
Houston, TX 77002
(713) 225-0321

Jefferson County Legal Aid Assn.
1200 Pearl Street
Court House Annex
Beaumont, TX 77701
(713) 835-8525

Laredo Legal Aid Society, Inc.
P.O. Box 1413
1102 Victoria
Laredo, TX 78040
(512) 722-7581

Lubbock Legal Services
1601 Metro Tower
Lubbock, TX 79401
(806) 763-4557

Legal Aid Society of Nueces County*
901 Leonard St.
Corpus Christi, TX 78401
(512) 888-0282

Community Action, Inc.
P.O. Box 644
415 S. Mitchell Street
San Marcos, TX 78666
(512) 392-1161

Tarrant County Legal Aid
  Foundation
406 W.T. Waggoner Bldg.
810 Houston Street
Fort Worth, TX 76102
(817) 334-1435

Texas Rural Legal Aid, Inc.*
103 East Third Street
Weslaco, TX 78596
(512) 968-9574

Legal Aid and Defender Society
  of Travis County
1713 East Sixth Street
Austin, TX 78702
(512) 476-6321

Waco-McLennan County Legal Aid
212 Community Services Bldg.
201 West Waco Drive
Waco, TX 76707
(817) 752-5596

---

*These legal aid services have several branch offices in various cities. Check your local
 telephone directory to determine whether there is a local branch, or call the number
 shown for information.

Appendix

Texas Consumer Agencies

Agency	Consumer Area
Attorney General's Office Consumer Protection Division P.O. Box 12548 Capitol Station Austin, TX 78711 (512) 475-3288	All consumer problems—deception, fraud
Dallas Regional Office 701 Commerce, Suite 200 Dallas, TX 75202 (214) 742-8944	
El Paso Regional Office 4824 Alberta Ave., Suite 160 El Paso, TX 79905 (915) 533-3484	
Houston Regional Office 723 Main, Suite 620 Houston, TX 77002 (713) 228-0701	
Lubbock Regional Office 806 Broadway, Suite 312 Lubbock, TX 79401 (806) 747-5238	

Agency	**Consumer Area**
McAllen Regional Office 4313 N. Tenth, Suite F McAllen, TX 78501 (512) 692-4547	
San Antonio Regional Office 200 Main Plaza, Suite 400 San Antonio, TX 78205 (512) 225-4191	
Consumer Credit Commissioner P.O. Box 2107 Austin, TX 78768 (512) 475-2111	Consumer loans; Retail transactions; Deception
Credit Union Department 1106 Clayton Lane Suite 206-East Twin Towers Bldg. Austin, TX 78723 (512) 475-2296	Credit Unions
Department of Agriculture Stephen F. Austin Bldg. Seventh Floor P.O. Box 12847 Capitol Station Austin, TX 78711 (512) 475-6346	Tests all consumer weighing devices and spot checks food items to make sure the price-weight conforms to actual weight; Receives and acts on complaints
Department of Banking 2601 North Lamar Austin, TX 78705 (512) 475-4451	Banking; Credit
Public Utility Commission of Texas Consumer Affairs Section 7800 Shoal Creek Boulevard Suite 450N Austin, TX 78757 (512) 475-7996	Public Utilities

Agency	Consumer Area
Railroad Commission of Texas P.O. Box 12967 Capitol Station Austin, TX 78711 (512) 475-2439	Gas Utilities
Savings and Loan Department 1004 Lavaca Austin, TX (512) 475-7991	Savings; Savings and loan institutions
State Securities Boards 709 L.B.J. Building P.O. Box 1316 Capitol Station Austin, TX 78711 (512) 475-4561 Houston Regional Office 3100 West Alabama, Suite 114 Houston, TX 77006 (713) 528-6128 Dallas Regional Office 312 Stemmons Tower East 2700 Stemmons Freeway Dallas, TX 75207 (214) 630-8681 Lubbock Regional Office Vickers Building 1507 13th Street Lubbock, TX 79401 (806) 762-8010	Stocks, bonds and investments
Texas Education Agency 201 East 11th Street Austin, TX 78711 (512) 457-3271	High School diploma plans; Correspondence schools; Vocational, business and trade schools
State Board of Insurance State Insurance Building 1110 San Jacinto Austin, TX 78786 (512) 475-2444	All types of insurance; Information on insurance programs and policies

Appendix

B

Federal Consumer Agencies

Agency	Consumer Area
Administration on Aging U.S. Department of HEW Washington, D.C. 20201	Problems of the aged: homemaker services; housing; legal problems; pensions Serves as federal government "clearinghouse" for all matters of concern to older people.
Agricultural Research Service U.S. Department of Agriculture Washington, D.C. 20250	Agriculture; budgets; children; clothing; family living; food; home economics; homemaking; housing Offers informative pamphlets free or for small charge on variety of subjects. Pamphlets can be obtained from County Agents.
Consumer and Marketing Service U.S. Department of Agriculture Washington, D.C. 20250	Farm products; food grades; food information; food stamps; meat inspection

Agency	**Consumer Area**
	Inspects meat in interstate commerce for wholesomeness; provides food grading system; safeguards fair competition in farm-products; provides money for free school meals programs; supplies food stamps; publishes bulletins on farm produce.
Consumer Protection and Environmental Health Services U.S. Department of HEW Washington, D.C. 20204	Environmental health; pollution; safety Provides information on pollution— some product safety. Deals with consumer problems.
Consumer Services U.S. Department of Agriculture Washington, D.C. 20025	Consumer goods; information services Furnishes information about consumer goods and services to all people.
Federal Communications Commission Washington, D.C. 20554	Radio; telegraph; telephone; television Regulates and licenses all communication industries including radio, telephone, telegraph, and television. Handles consumer complaints and recommendations.
Federal Extension Service Department of Agriculture Washington, D.C. 20250	Agriculture; appliances; children; family living; farming; food; home economics; money management; nutrition; textiles; clothing Provides out-of-school education and information on homemaking, home economics, farming agriculture and all related areas.
Federal Housing Administration Washington, D.C. 20410	Housing—construction; design; mortgages Insures mortgages so that homes may be purchased or improved by eligible persons.

Agency	**Consumer Area**
	Deals with consumer complaints where houses being built do not meet specifications.
Federal Trade Commission Sixth and Pennsylvania Ave. S.W. Washington, D.C. 20580 (202) 655-4000 Dallas Regional Office 2001 Bryan St. Dallas, Texas 75201 (214) 749-3057	Advertising; deception; fraud; Guarantees; monopolies; packaging Prevents false and deceptive advertising, sale of dangerous products, misbranding, and restraint of trade. Investigates complaints related to the above areas—interstate transactions only.
Food and Drug Administration 5600 Fishers Lane Rockville, Maryland 20852 Houston Regional Office 515 Rusk Houston, TX 77002 (713) 226-4397	Safety in cosmetics, drugs and foods. Handles consumer protection in marketing of drugs, foods, cosmetics, potentially hazardous consumer products—handles consumer complaints on impurities.
National Highway Traffic Safety Administration 400 Seventh St. S.W. Washington, D.C. 20590	Auto safety; highway safety; traffic pattern safety Sets standards for traffic safety, auto safety, and highway safety.
Office of Economic Opportunity 1200 19th Street, N.W. Washington, D.C. 20506	Auto purchasing; contracts; consumer education; credit; discrimination; family counseling; food buying; furniture buying; household appliances; job discrimination; legal aid; shopping guide; TV purchasing Helps low income, disadvantaged to stay out of poverty or to get out of it.
Office of Consumer Affairs U.S. Department of HEW Washington, D.C. 20201	Consumer rights; drugs; foods Actively seeks consumer participation in developing a Food and Drug Administration program to respond to consumer needs and rights.

Agency	Consumer Area
Securities and Exchange Commission Washington, D.C. 20549	Bonds; stocks Protects consumers by regulating the issuance and trading of stocks and bonds—publishes consumer information pamphlets.
Superintendent of Documents U.S. Government Printing Office Washington, D.C. 20402	Consumer bibliography; documents; mailing list of government publications; pamphlets; public information Provides low-cost, information publications for public—circulates free mailing list.
U.S. Postal Service 475 L'Enfant Plaza West S.W. Washington, D.C. 20260	Mail Fraud; obscene mail
Women's Bureau U.S. Dept. of Labor Washington, D.C. 20210 Dallas Regional Office 555 Griffin Sq. Bldg. Dallas, TX 75202	Working women Publishes information on working women—deals with the problems of women workers.

Index